WILLIAM BALLENY HOWDEN

The Triumphs and Tears of an Australian Pioneer

Ian C. Howden

BALBOA.
PRESS
A DIVISION OF HAY HOUSE

Balboa Press books may be ordered through booksellers or by contacting:

Balboa Press
A Division of Hay House
1663 Liberty Drive
Bloomington, IN 47403
www.balboapress.com.au
1 (877) 407-4847

Print information available on the last page.

ISBN: 978-1-5043-0641-6 (sc)
ISBN: 978-1-5043-0642-3 (e)

Balboa Press rev. date: 02/02/2017

The notes that I prepared about the life of W B Howden were in episode form for a family reunion. They would have remained as such had it not been for my granddaughters who persuaded me that I should publish the story of their courageous ancestor. I therefore devote this work to my lovely granddaughters.

Contents

William Balleny Howden and the years in which he was Shire President of Alberton Shire Council

Prologue and Acknowledgements

WB Howden stands like a giant at the head of a long line of descendants. He made the decision to leave a comfortable family life in Edinburgh and travelled to a country that offered none of the comforts to which he had become accustomed. Yet he overcame these extreme early difficulties and crafted a life to which he attracted his whole family from Edinburgh. His strength of character is to be admired and emulated by his many descendants living in Australia and other parts of the world.

I have enjoyed putting together the story of his life. In doing so I have kept true to the pathway of his life and I have tried to imagine the emotions that he experienced throughout the changing stages and experiences.

There were some movements in the life of William Balleny that were not clear and I have included the story with the barest of background knowledge. Other members of the family may be able to correct what I have included and I will be very pleased to receive their comments. I include my comments on some of these periods.

After arriving in Sydney, my assumption that he travelled North with Robert Issell Perrot is based on the record in the diary by John Riddell of the voyage on the "Abberton". WB and Perrot had obviously made friends on the voyage and Riddell commented that they had travelled North together. I followed this up at the University library in Armadale and found many references to Perrot but nothing of Howden. I have therefore suggested that WB went north but did not stay for long.

How WB made it to Victoria is not clear. I found no record of his travel by ship. There is a comment in Charles Daley's book "The Story of Gippsland" that Harvey and Howden had a run at Gelantipy, and my sister, Shirley, believes that he settled there for a short time on his way down from Sydney, possibly with McMillan. An alternative may be that he later bought this land as speculation that all the trading between Tasmania and Sydney would come through Port Albert and carried by bullock or horse drawn wagon to Sydney. My father did say that WB did speculate by purchasing land on a track from Port Albert to Sydney at likely stage distances of the wagons.

There are different opinions about his presence on the "Singapore" that was chartered to salvage the goods from the "Clonmel" wreck in 1841. The name of Hawden is listed on that voyage and my father told me that he first went to Port Albert to salvage a ship wreck. Esme Rash, the historian at Port Albert Museum, considers that names were often spelt incorrectly on the manifest of ships. It is therefore very likely that the name of Hawden should have been Howden especially since the chartering of the "Singapore" was a very hastily arranged voyage.

Before WB was married to Sarah Cooper I believe that he did try to persuade a lady named Kathleen to settle with him in Port Albert. The support for that is that his name is linked to her on a voyage from Melbourne to Port Albert. The episode with the elephant that I have woven into that part of history was reported in the Alberton papers at the same period as Kathleen stayed with WB.

The marriage certificate of Sarah Cooper and WB initiated

a search that revealed that Sarah had been married to James Leage, they were not divorced but had drifted apart. We can only assume that WB and Sarah drifted apart also as we were not able to find divorce papers. Where Sarah finished up is an unsolved mystery, in spite of hours of detective work by a number of family members.

My brother Rob Howden initiated my writing attempts when he asked me to put together some of the experiences of our ancestor's early life in Australia. I Acknowledge the great help I have received from my sister Shirley Howden who meticulously collected the historical facts of the Howden family. She has also scanned the draft copies of each episode and has ensured that I have not wandered too far from the truth in my endeavours to interpret how WB would have been thinking and feeling during the phases of his life's journey. She loaned a number of books about the pioneers of Gippsland from her library. Shirley also created the section about Agnes from her research of the Duncan family. I hope that you will agree that the WB story would not be complete without this chapter.

Ann Wilkinson (Nee Anne Balleny Howden - Rev William Balleny Howden - James Archibald Howden) gave me copies of her father's "Life Story" and "The Howden Story in Scotland and Victoria", and Trevor Howden provided some photographs. I also obtained a copy of the passage diary of John Carre Riddell who was one of the 30 passengers on the "Abberton" along with William Balleny.

Esme Rash, the historian of the Port Albert Museum, provided a mountain of information in the form of newspaper reports, business documents images and letters. It was mainly from these intimate documents that I was able to know WB and Agnes and their immediate family. I have endeavoured to use this information to create the William Balleny Howden story.

The museum at Port Albert has a large store of background information and detail about the Howden family. There is far more there than I was able to glean in the two or three days that I spent there.

Using the background from books and Google also helped to recreate the atmosphere at the time. I am sure that some of my living relatives had more accessible information about the experiences with our great grandparents WB and Agnes through their own grandparents. My grandfather was Robert Charles who died when my father, Roland, was only 12 years old. Personal links direct to WB were therefore not as strong as some others who had a more intimate link to our hero. I hope that you will excuse some of my attempts to paint the picture of our family history when your experience differs from my own.

Ian C. Howden

What I left behind

May I introduce myself to you all, I am William Balleny Howden, and as an impatient and rebellious youth I left a potentially comfortable life in Scotland for the promise of creating an exciting future on the other side of the world. From the moment the sails unfurled on the good ship Abberton my adventure started. Regrets I have none for I have experienced all of the passions that life can reveal. Great joy, sadness beyond belief, loneliness, camaraderie, success, and the glue through it all; love. Now, as the thrill of adventure has long since escaped me I have the desire to tell you all about it. I was the first of a generation of the Howden family who came to the Colony of New South Wales and settled in the town of Port Albert, Gippsland. I hope that members of the extended family will understand how they became Australians.

The cold winters of Scotland are no time to come into this world, but January 26th in the year 1816, mother decided it was time. The house was certainly kept warm with fires in the important rooms throughout the house, and I did not have to face the fierce cold that many others less fortunate had to endure.

Our family were able to afford the luxury of a fine home, thanks to our forefathers who built a profitable watchmaking and jewellery business in Edinburgh. Before I tell you my story, let me tell you something of my father and grandfather.

Grandfather James started as an apprenticed watchmaker in 1764 at the age of 15. He died three years before I was born. After 7 years with Alexander Farquharson grandfather transferred to James Cowan to serve out his indenture. In November 1771 he completed his indenture and moved into his own shop and there started what became a very successful family clock making and jewellery business.

They say in real estate that the 3 key issues are position, position and position. Grandfather obviously knew about it when he chose Hunter Square on the corner of High St and South Bridge to launch his career. To this day this continues as one of the busiest parts of Edinburgh. Not satisfied with being an indentured Watchmaker he continued study until he presented his essay to the essay masters in 1775 for the highest qualification in watchmaking.

Grandfather worked diligently and his reputation as an excellent watchmaker grew along with his business that he passed on to my father, James, and my uncle William in 1808. The advertising and reports in Edinburgh journals including one on Scottish clockmakers have praised James Howden in Hunter Square in glowing terms such as "-- there was not a better known business in Edinburgh than that of James Howden".

Although father finished his watchmaking indentures in London before returning to work with grandfather, he did not take over management of the shop until five years later, by which time he had also produced his essay and obtained the same high watchmaking qualification as my grandfather. Uncle William also completed his indentures in London as a jeweller and silversmith and had to have some years of experience in the shop before the two were given joint ownership. The tradition of quality was firmly instilled into the two young managers and no advertising was ever allowed to make such comment as "moderate prices". "cheap" never entered their head, instead their advertisements were "--3 Hunter Square beg to announce that their stock of watches, jewellery, silver plate, cutlery etc. --will be found to be extensive and of the best quality."

The firm of J and W Howden had outgrown the Hunter Square shop before I was born and they moved almost across the road to 9 South Bridge. This was only a short 5 minute walk from our home in Buccleuch Place, and I remember walking to the shop with mother as a young boy. By the time that I was 8, Father and Uncle William had been managing the shoptogether for fifteen years and they decided to go separate ways. Father moved his watchmaking business further along South Bridge to No.56 New Buildings, North Bridge St. The new shop was much larger and the watch making and watch repair business was "---one of the best establishments in town." Many people who came to our home commented on the quality of the clocks and how clever it was to make them; I was very proud of my father. The three shops the family had were all within a stone throw of the busy corner of High St and where South Bridge changed to North Bridge. I am sure that this contributed to the success of the business. Yes, my forebears were not only good watchmakers but also good businessmen. I left you a while back with my mother and the midwife while I spoke to you about my father and grandfather. Mother and father did not waste time having me christened. Born on January 26th and christened on March 1st, yes, in the same year. Of course I was Baptised in the Church of Scotland Kirk, St Cuthbert's, a church popular with the freemen at the time. It was about one mile from our home, a short walk but not entirely level. The church has a history that dates back to 1127 when King David 1 gave the land below Edinburgh Castle to St Cuthbert's.

Number 3 Hunter St . Ann Wilkinson in foreground. (nee Ann Balleny Howden, W. B.(Bill) Howden, James Howden)

As I grew I was able to play in the common that was at the end of our street. Fortunately the city fathers had enough foresight to maintain possession of this land which is now being developed into a fine parkland. I went to school at the church school and hence was well schooled in the Presbyterian theology and the strict way of life. My Mother certainly taught us what was right and wrong and I quickly learned not to step into the wrong area. With 5 children under the age of 10, mother certainly was kept busy but I did not appreciate the stress that my siblings and I put on her until I had a family of my own. Mother died eight days after Janet was born and I suspect that was why Janet was named after my mother. I was then the second oldest at seven, James was nine, Ann five and Andrew three. Life changed suddenly after mother died and father spent much more time with us than he had previously. We were looked after by two servants who lived with us in the house.

Brother James, who was to be heir to the family watchmaking business was drowned at sea before commencing his indentures.

When visiting the shop in North Bridge, I got to know the senior watchmaker, Mr Brown. He was a friend of the family and often came to our home. Mr Brown had worked for father for a long time and when I was 12 years old Father made him a partner of the business and changed the name to Howden and Company.

Another major change was the move to 25 Windsor St, a much larger house in a fashionable area with wide streets but not close to the large parkland I was used to playing in. It was still close to the church and to father's business but on the other side of town. St Cuthbert's as it is today, and although there was an upgrading in the late 19th century and again in 1990 it is much the same as when William Balleny was Christened. It stands in large grounds and in the shadow of the Edinburgh Castle.

Throughout my school years, sport was a higher priority to me than academic study. In an effort to encourage me into the business, father gave me work to do in the shop, but accompanying him to London on buying visits was much more to my liking. London opened my eyes to broader possibilities in life that were infinitely more appealing than watchmaking.

The newspapers contained interesting stories about some of the colonies in the new world and the government were encouraging people to move to a number of far-away places. Many Scottish people had taken the plunge and I talked about it with my friends. While together we were full of enthusiasm and youthful ambition to launch into an adventure of discovery in a new world. I was the only one who resisted the dampening influence of family whose reaction was like Jesus parable of the brambles that choked the sown seed.

I gathered as much information as I could from newspapers, journals, books and talking with anyone who had knowledge about these new places offering exciting opportunities. Finally, I decided that Australia was to be my destiny and I drew the family into discussions on the subject. Father listened patiently but James and Andrew could see only all of the dangers. Ann was enthusiastic in support and she carried along the sixteen year old Janet when we were discussing my ideas. The two girls could always win over father and I am sure that their support finally influenced father who offered to assist with my preparations.

I had saved some money and felt that I had satisfied the family, so I started looking for ships sailing to Australia. I chose the "Abberton", due to sail from London on 15th April 1839. It is a 451 Ton three mast square rigged ship and on this voyage it was due to carry sheep from the Scottish Moors, general cargo, 25 officers and crew and 36 passengers.

The Journey

When I look back on the moment that the ship's mooring ropes were cast off my mind raced. It was like taking one large step from security into insecurity, like stepping off the end of the pier with no life buoy and only a rudimentary knowledge of swimming.

I was older than the young Queen Victoria who was only 20 when the Abberton sailed from Gravesend. London was a rapidly growing city and the centre of a revolution in manufacturing, transport, finance and of the expanding English global possessions. The flood of people moving to London had caused problems of poverty and crime that had been addressed by creating a London Police Force ("Bobbies") and sending criminals to New South Wales .I was encouraged by the fact that a group of influential people led by James Macarthur had persuaded the Parliament to stop the Transport of prisoners to NSW only last year. They pinned their hope of developing a colony based on free immigration rather than "Transportation". Governor Bourke had already given prisoners in NSW more freedom before he retired last year, and it appeared to me that New South Wales showed promise of emerging from the descriptive tag of "dunghill of the Empire".

The farewell with my friends in Edinburgh is faint in my mind which indicates that it was not a swell or boisterous affair. What I can remember is the clip clop of the horses hooves that clings to my brain along with the leaden silence in the coach as the family accompanied me to the ship. The coach was not large and our bodies swayed almost in tune with the surging emotions of the five family members. The earlier family discussions about my decision were forgotten. Drowned out by prolonged hugs followed by waves and shouts from ship to shore and from shore to ship. Then the mooring lines slipped into the water and the ship slowly parted company with the wharf and the emotions on the shore. April 15th 1839 was a day to remember.

I looked over the rail of the ship at the water that was contaminated with sewerage and an associated stench. The Thames was rapidly being killed by the overloaded sewerage system, and I was glad to be leaving this behind. The ship weaved its way slowly through the congested waters of the Thames to the open waters of the Channel. Immediately we had a baptism of what to expect over the next four months. There were high winds for three days and we had reached only Downes, where we had to anchor in open sea. The winds were so strong that night that all hands and the passengers were on deck as there was a real danger of drifting with a consequent wrecking of the ship.

The captain blamed the pilot for the bad choice of anchorage and next day he was replaced with a new pilot who sailed us into a much better anchorage. A doctor joined the ship for the journey which certainly made Mrs Darby happy as she gave birth to a daughter soon after the doctor's arrival on board. In fact, the bad weather between Gravesend and Downes had severely tested the seasickness resistance of all of the passengers and the doctor's presence was appreciated.

The winds were still unfavourable and it was ten days after leaving London that we reached the Isle of Wright. By this time I was getting used to the tiny cabin and the dull routine of eating and drinking. Breakfast at eight thirty, lunch at twelve thirty, tea at three thirty, dinner at eight thirty and brandy and water at nine thirty. For those who wanted it there was abundant Malt, Port and Sherry. After that most of us turned in for the night. Fortunately, the people were all easy to get along with and the families with children tried to keep the young ones occupied so that they were not interfering with the comfort of others.

Two more days of favourable winds and we passed Start Point and headed south, away from good old England. Unfortunately, Mrs. Darby was very ill at that stage and the hot weather did not help her condition.

The cook was a black man who was not well organised until we reached the Bay of Biscay. There we met a French fishing boat and were fed some fine meals of mackerel, eggs, barley broth and finished off with currants, almonds and raisins. We stayed in the bay for two days to take on provisions which gave the cook an opportunity to get his galley in order. From then on our meals improved.

April 28th was a Sunday and the first mate read prayers and we sang some hymns. The informal atmosphere was certainly different to St Cuthbert's but bible readings and hymns turned my thoughts to home and Edinburgh.

On the 30th we left the Bay of Biscay with very favourable winds. The porpoises played beside the ship and a couple of the men fired at them unsuccessfully with a harpoon. As we approached Gibraltar Poor Mrs Darby became dangerously ill and by the time that we reached Madeira she was near death. The doctor and the captain decided that there was nothing more could be done for her and we sailed past the island. Next day she was buried in a watery grave after a short and emotional service by the captain.

Having sailed past the Madeira Islands and the Canary Island without going ashore we all looked forward to the Cape Verde Islands, for the captain had promised time ashore at the port of Praia on the Island of Santiago. Although I was disappointed not to have stopped at the Canary Islands it was grand to see the dominant mountain peak, Tenarife, as we sailed past the main Canary Island.

It took the Abberton a week to sail from the Canary Islands to the promised visit ashore at Santiago and while most of the passengers kept to themselves during this fair weather sailing, I found Mrs French and Miss Gore were quite flirtatious. It was flattering to be singled out for their attention, and I found out that I was not the only one. When the men retired together in the evenings the conversation often was about their flirting and our imagination created some wild stories as to why two ladies alone should be going to Sydney.

There was abundant time for discussion and voicing opinion on all subjects, but the majority of the time was spent airing our ambitions for when we arrived in New south Wales. This was good for all of us as it broadened our horizons considerably. The one common trait in all discussions was the confidence that everyone had of achieving success.

We anchored in the Bay of Praia, Santiago on May 12th to the news that the SS Red Rover had been wrecked under suspicious circumstances on 24th April. Her bow was still visible and it was obviously the most convenient place to be wrecked for salvage afterwards. All of the 70 cabin passengers were saved by the SS Ferguson which was also moored in the port. The passengers were still at the port and were in a most distressed state of mind. The Consul was arranging for most to return to England, except for 3 cabin and 2 steerage passengers who decided to join the Abberton. They told us that Red Rover was originally a convict ship sailing between England and Tasmania and was later used as a female emigrant ship before transporting paying passengers and general cargo to Sydney.

When we went ashore in the small boats the waves upset the overcrowded vessels and we all received an unexpected dunking, but there were no injuries. This did not dampen our enthusiasm to enjoy the 2-day shore visit. We were invited to many houses to find the families and pigs all living together in the same dwelling, even though the families were supposed to be very rich. The fruit on Santiago was abundant and delicious, mainly oranges and bananas. When it came time to return to the Abberton we found that as well as the five new passengers we had the company of a bull. I do not know who arranged for the bull to be added to our farmyard, but it was later the subject of an interesting business deal by one of our passengers. He bought the bull on the condition that it arrived in Sydney alive and well. The seller claimed that it had a pedigree, which I doubt, but the buyer considered that if the pedigree meant nothing then he could sell the bull to a butcher and recoup some of the cost. The transaction was the subject of considerable conjecture and joking on many nights round the dining table; and after dinner when the men got together.

The tropics introduced us to a cocktail of weather wonders; oppressive heat, becalmed for two days, a lightning display accompanied by the Gods of Thunder and water from the sky as if the heavens had been opened. Oh that it could have been watched in comfort instead of being tossed like a cork in the wild seas whipped up by the storm.

We crossed the equator in the midst of a storm so that

the crossing ceremony was postponed for a day. Two of the crew dressed up as Mr and Mrs Neptune and set about dunking everybody with sea water. Seven of us volunteered to be blindfolded, shaved and dunked and dunked again. "Mrs Neptune" insisted on repeatedly hugging us in a "fond" embrace which left us scratched by her "beard" made of leather and hair pins. Even though we had no ills the doctor insisted on the "taking of pills" which did not appear to have any subsequent after effects. This involved all of the passengers and was all part of the ceremony. The seven of us were " washed" with flour and water and fun was had by all. In fact, this playfulness bonded us together, as the oppressive heat had played on the tempers of the passengers and crew alike.

Having survived all that the tropics could serve, there was a period of full sails and a return to the routine. For almost a week I enjoyed many hours reading "Oliver Twist" which had been a serial in "Bentley's Miscellany" since 1936 and only recently had been published in book form. One of the families had a copy that they generously circulated. Charles Dickens gave us all background to another life in the London to which we had recently waved goodbye.

It was 19th June and only a little over two months out when the captain ordered only a quarter pint of water for washing per day. We could not understand why we did not call into the port of Cape Town to replenish our water and food supply. A passing Dutch ship that had left Amsterdam four weeks after us drew abreast and we sent across a small boat for some potatoes and biscuits, but no rice as I had hoped. The Dutch ship was much faster than the Abberton and it soon left us in its wake.

Under the circumstances we could not complain about the food for the cabin passengers had fresh mutton and pork daily. The steerage passengers were supplied with food that they had to cook themselves in very crowded communal conditions. Some of their space had been taken up with cargo. They had to bring their own bedding and they slept, ate and socialised in the same space. Steerage passengers were often confined to the lower deck for days during rough weather and the cabin passengers did not mix freely with them. Of the 16 steerage passengers there were only three women who must have found it extremely difficult living for so long in this cramped communal area.

There were 25 adult cabin passengers and eight children, fourteen passengers were single men, there were three married couples and five unattached ladies. Had the conditions been more pleasant I am sure that this group of people would have existed together quite happily. Unfortunately, tempers wore thin, particularly when we were confined below decks in rough weather and some of the men drank heavily. Water for washing was now completely forbidden and there were still six weeks of sailing before we reached Sydney.

The unaccompanied ladies mixed more frequently with the single men as the voyage progressed, but there is always someone who abuses a perfectly good arrangement. The captain made an example of Miss Gore for her alleged impropriety by banning her from the cuddy table. The fault lay mainly with the ship's mates who encouraged her to act with some lack of decorum on occasions. The action by the captain against Miss Gore incited ten of the single men to form a club with Mr Dalzell as chairman. The purpose was to consider matters of importance to take to the captain and to organise activities to while away the time. Their intentions were made known to all passengers and crew in this declaration.

"Our aim is to pass away the tedious hours by harmless mirth and glee and to suppress any vice and immorality which may appear on board, and in after years when we meet in a

foreign land to look back and congratulate each other over porter to the mast head on the many hairbreadth escapes which have been made from informers and all other evil disposed persons while we were on board"

After rounding the Cape we had about thirty days of good sailing, but the sea was not going to let us off without showing us what it really can do. For three days we were under reefed main topsail and foresail and every part of the ship was swimming with water. Every wave washed over the decks and some of the waves threatened to smash the vessel in two. The crew had great difficulty in making sail and other adjustments. The passengers were thrown about onto furniture and walls like leaves in the wind, but were able to avoid any serious injury.

After this the weather varied for the next ten days until we were off Cape Leeuwin and only 1500 miles to Sydney. Seven days of good sailing weather brought us to Cape Otway but Bass Strait was not going to let us through without recourse to much tacking and little progress for three days.

Leaving in our wake a group of Islands named the Kent group we sailed north up the New South Wales coast. The weather was clear and sunny, better than any that we had experienced in the past four months. This being the Southern Hemisphere winter we looked forward to considerable improvement compared with the cold climate of Scotland.

On Tuesday August 20th the Abberton anchored within half a mile of Sydney. At seven in the evening the passengers landed on unsteady sea legs that had us all walking like drunken sailors. That night I luxuriated in a hot bath and I felt that four months of difficult times came out of the pores of my skin with all of the unwashed grime.

On the next day there was a rush for a paper to find out what news we could and the possibilities that lay before us.

On the 22ⁿᵈ the papers reported our arrival in Sydney and I found that the Sydney Herald had given me a wife overnight. I preferred the passenger list in the gazette which reported my arrival as a single man.

Everywhere we walked there was excited conversation, not only with our fellow passengers, but also with established New South Welsh people. They were hungry for the latest news from home and we were hungry for knowledge about our new home. The newspaper gave us the journalists slant on events but we wanted to hear what the people had to say. They could relate to our emotions on arrival and we were anxious to hear their stories and where to go from here.

Learning A New Lifestyle

I look back at the time of my arrival in Australia and the first 17 months before I had the good fortune to be able to join a fine group of pioneers in the Gipps Land Company. I realise that it was not only my life that was going through a dramatic change, but so was the colony of Australia. It was a watershed period for the country and for me.

The population in Australia was 131,000 in 1841and about 35,000 of that were clustered in Sydney. Melbourne was still a small town of 4,000 that was being starved of funds for infrastructure such as roads by the authorities in Sydney. Queen Victoria did not grant her name to a southern colony separated from New South Wales until August 1850. At the same time South Australia and Van Diemen's Land were also given the opportunity to form their own government.

These decisions, made in England, were not the only ones to bring changes in direction. I have already mentioned that England abolished slavery, and there were now influential voices saying that the assignment of convicts was a form of slavery. This resulted in a fall in the number of convicts arriving in Australia from 3427 in 1837 to 2293 arrivals in 1839. During the equivalent years the number of free immigrants rose from 4275 to 13,358. This trend caused changes in the economy as pastoralists, merchants and shopkeepers had to pay for their labour instead of free labour by convicts. There was an inevitable decline in profits and an outcry from farmers and businessmen alike.

But let me tell you my story about the intervening years between when I arrived in Sydney and arriving in Port Albert.

On the ship, Robert Issell Perrot and I, being of similar age, had found common ground. He was known by his second name and we had agreed to find lodgings together in Sydney until we decided where our future lay. Accommodation was plentiful but the quality varied from good to terrible. We were recommended a small hotel on the outskirts of the town that was comfortable and enabled us to share a room. Breakfast was included in the price and other meals were served as an extra on request. This proved to be a good base to start the Australian adventure.

I remember vividly the surprise that I had to see such development in the short space of 50 years since settlement by Governor Philip with convicts and army personnel in 1788. Sydney was a large busy town that reminded me of portions of Edinburgh, with many good buildings but few with any pretensions of architectural beauty. George Street was at least a mile of shops that attracted the ladies of all sections of the community as they moved from shop to shop. They travelled upon wheels of all descriptions, from the showy closed carriages to the humble chaise or gig. Very few ladies rode horses, although there was a well publicised horse race from Hyde Park to Botany for lady riders and with the prize of a side saddle. The runner up claimed she was beaten only because the winner swerved into her path close to the finish.

Macquarie Street had most of the government buildings and

churches, the Hospital, the Hyde Park Barracks, the Supreme Court, the Government House Stables, St James Church of England and St Mary's Cathedral. Although designed in 1821 by Francis Greenway, Government House had not progressed at the same speed as the other buildings. Instead it stood alone, partly built, while English Parliament decided that an ex-convict could not design the Governor's residence. The abandoned construction had to await much red tape in England and the arrival in New South Wales of an English designer.

In the first few days, the small, but important things in life dominated our thoughts. The abundant supply of water was a luxury after the limited allowance on board ship. It was fresh, clean and without being flavoured by the casks of vinegar or rum, and without having to be left to settle. Every action in life was an enjoyment, I could walk without the floor moving about, both hands were free to shave and I could set my wine glass on the table without fear of the contents finishing up in my plate.

Vegetables, after a long diet of pork and rice, were most welcome, but most fruit at the time were out of season. It was not long before we were able to enjoy some wonderful new fruit flavours. Melons were huge, about 18 inches in diameter, and the greengrocers stacked them in piles like large cannon balls.

Not every part of our initiation to Australia was pleasant. Flies swarmed in their tens of thousands and blackened the dinner table as soon as the food appeared. Mosquitoes may have been less in numbers but they were far more of a problem as they insisted on attaching themselves to our bodies, leaving an irritating reminder of their presence. At night it was necessary to protect ourselves against their attacks, and instead of the four poster bed I was used to, each bed was decked with a fine net suspended on the ceiling at a single point and tucked round the edge of the bed. Before settling down, it was necessary to first ensure that there were no insect intruders beneath the netting, tuck the netting securely under the mattress, leave a small untucked area to dive through, and then secure that piece under the mattress.

Issell and I decided that we would not immediately look for work, but would orient ourselves first. The taverns would be the obvious place to find some local flavour, and Issell, who had a military background, was certainly the leader in this direction, while I was the inexperienced hanger on. It certainly was not hard to find a tavern, but our favorite was the Hero of Waterloo, situated near the military barracks. Issell was also attracted to it because he related to the clientele of mostly military personnel, and they were of the same age group as we were. I must admit that the conversation was of a considerably coarser nature than I had been used to, either at home or on board ship, where the presence of ladies restricted unbridled smut. It was inevitable that a group of young men in their early twenties would soon turn their conversation to the fair sex. We learned that although the ratio of male to female had improved from 7 to one to a more even 4 to one, the eligible ladies were all accounted for, or if not they were completely fenced off by their parents. Although this could have been disturbing conversation for a 23 year old, it did not rate highly in my ambition while I had no idea where my long term direction would be.

We were to find that class distinction had developed in Australia even greater than in England. The aborigines were the lowest end of the scale, much lower than the convicts, and at the highest end were the wealthy settlers who had attached themselves to the Governor's parties and social events in Sydney. Although there were a surprising number of emancipists who had become wealthy, they were not able to break into the social set of the wealthy free settlers.

On Sunday my training back home at St Cuthbert's had engrained the habit of attending church and I found Scots church on the corner of Jamieson St and York St was a large and friendly congregation. Surprisingly Issell was very willing to accompany me and we learned a lot by talking with the friendly congregation. The Minister, John Dunmore Lang, had come out from Scotland in 1823 when he was only aged 24. The Rev Lang had become a very respected identity in the whole of New South Wales and over a wide range of the community. He had built the church within a year of his arrival in Sydney. His sermons were long and tedious and he could on occasions speak with fire and brimstone. His real success was that he had accumulated a friendly group of largely Scottish immigrants whose accent was familiar to my ears. Scots church became a home away from home during my short stay in Sydney. Rev Lang's success was encouraging to a young Scot like myself who was seeking success in a very different environment to which I was accustomed.

After a few days gathering our land legs and a considerable store of information, we were confident to arrange the loan of two horses to explore beyond the immediate surroundings of the city.

Our first venture was to the lighthouse at South Head. Ships entering the harbour were first sighted by the lighthouse keeper who transmitted the news to the authorities in Sydney by messenger. With the road between the lighthouse and Sydney providing an important link it was understandable that it was well defined and well maintained. There were some areas of the road that were very stony, with areas of rock outcrops that were very slippery. Fortunately, the horses were far more accustomed to these conditions than we were and we soon learned to follow their instinct rather than to follow our own.

Most of the growth along the way was tea-tree and some of the spring flowers were putting on an early display that promised to blossom into a spectacular ground cover. Dominant among the tree growth were the acacia which were abundant and in full bloom. The locals had renamed this golden flowered tree the Wattle.

Parrots of the most brilliant hue regularly crossed our path with noisy banter. Most interesting was a flock of black cockatoos that had taken command on a dead eucalypt. Their heads moved wisely from side to side as they eyed our progress. When they decided that we were of no interest to them they displayed an impressive red flash in their tail feathers as they departed.

Arrival at the lighthouse was spectacular, not for the structure, but for the ocean view from the elevated position above the seas pounding on the rocks below and booming like thunder. Opposite, the corresponding cliff called North Head formed the most stupendous gates to the harbour.

On our return we took the opportunity to ride through the Domain that was favoured by Lady Macquarie during the reign of Governor Macquarie from 1810 to 1821. She regularly sat on a carved rock looking across Farm Cove and the opposite banks of the harbour. The dignified and extremely beautiful Domain by day became the meeting place of the housemaids and their boyfriends by night.

Our next venture was to ride out to Parramatta, the country home of the Governor. The main part of the road was bad beyond belief. Two years of desolating drought had preceded our arrival in Sydney and the dust blown by the wind and passing carriages settled everywhere and restricted our breathing. The first gang of convicts chained together and working on the road was a stark reminder that although Australia was emerging from the original status as a penal settlement there were still many yet to complete their terms of imprisonment. There were also new prisoners yet to arrive. We were to learn that similar gangs were a common sight throughout New South Wales.

Parramatta Road contributed handsomely to the large number of taverns in Sydney and it's surrounds, and we made good use of their facilities before arriving in Parramatta.

Parramatta was a straggling and extensive place with wide streets, containing houses and shops of every size and description. Orange groves and vineyards abounded. We took the opportunity to view the country residence of Governor Gipps. It was indeed a worthy residence for the Governor with its extensive open surrounding area, and it gave us a feeling of pride for our adopted country.

I can remember vividly the long ride back to Sydney because it was the first time that Issell and I had discussed at length what our next moves should be. We had enjoyed the few weeks since taking leave of the ship. Those days had been like an adventure holiday with fascinating new experiences everywhere we turned. Each facet of Sydney life had been stored in our minds creating a sound platform for deciding where we were going to fit into this raw new community. Neither of us was impressed by the continuous drunken, boisterous behaviour round the 250 or more taverns in the Sydney area.

There were openings for employment with merchants, and in some of the taverns. Our chances of being granted land were not good because neither of us had farming experience, or the advantage of connections in England or with the New South Wales Legislative Council. Issell, with his background in military service, was leaning towards applying for one of the jobs in the NSW Police Force. I was undecided but I knew that we had reached the time for decisions if we were to survive. The long ride out to Parramatta and back, with heavy discussion on the return journey, had made us too tired for decisions of such importance. It was as if the past weeks had been a dress rehearsal, every detail had been practiced and tomorrow the curtain would rise for a grand opening; we hoped.

4

The New England Experiment

When we met in the morning to consolidate our deliberations of the previous day, I was not surprised that Issell had decided to apply for a position as a Police Supervisor in New England, about 200 miles north of Sydney. My background certainly did not qualify me for a similar job, neither did my inclination. I was not attracted to Sydney, a town that had developed harsh reactions to the unruly nature of the community. I was attracted to the magnificent harbour scenery but I abhorred the life style that reminded me of the docklands of London. Like Issell, I wanted to experience life at the fringes of development where small communities were developing their own character and I wanted to be part of that development. The area chosen by Issell was new but had recently experienced severe conflict between the settlers and the aborigines, leading to a massacre of the aborigines.

It happened at Myall Creek over 250 miles north of Sydney in a northern part of the recently opened New England area. John Fleming, the son of a local squatter, initiated the incident. He gathered eleven of the convicts working on his father's property and set out on a killing spree of peaceful aboriginals. They killed 28 men women and children, dragged them to a central area, and built a fire on the pile of bodies. Over a period of three months the 11 convicts were arrested and committed to trial in November. Fleming was not arrested. At the end of the hearing the jury had not left the chambers more than five minutes when they returned to give a "not guilty" verdict, with the explanation that they "were not prepared to convict any white man just because he had killed some blacks". Governor Gipps was appalled at the decision; attorney Plungket insisted that all human life was equal and he recalled the convicts for retrial. Four of the group were convicted and hung in February while the others were set free.

The actions of the convicts, the decisions of the jury, the attorney, and all other players in this "massacre" were discussed over and over on many occasions and it left a lasting impression on me and I am sure on Issell, who later became a police magistrate in the New England district.

This was the worst of a number of isolated incidents in the New England area that led Governor Gipps to order the formation of Police Supervisors and thus gave Issell his opportunity. The Supervisors were each given a group of mounted and armed convicts to patrol the New England Area. Convicts had to be used at the time because this was the only labour available.

IsselI successfully applied for a Police Supervisor's position centred at Armidale. Through one of the Sydney merchants I was offered the opportunity to travel to Armidale with two wagons of supplies for the district. Issell had to report to a police commissioner in Armidale. The supplies for which I was responsible were to be delivered to the property of a Mr Dumaresq, a leading pastoralist whose homestead was also the local store for the surrounding area.

At a time in my life when I should have been making positive decisions about a future career, I had to ask myself why I should endure an extremely uncomfortable week on a supply wagon to a destination of questionable repute and no foreseeable potential for me?.

I was influenced by the horrific incident that had become known as the "Myall Creek Massacre", and by the conflicting arguments that ebbed and flowed in every hotel bar, church and family. Friends and families were divided in support and against Fleming and the convicted convicts. The four convicts were hung 6 months prior to our arrival, but the populace of Sydney had such a variety of views it was still a popular subject of extremely vigorous conversation.

It had been estimated at the time that there were 4,380 people "beyond the boundaries of Sydney", one third of them were convicts still to serve out their term. There were 250,000 cattle and over 2 million sheep. New England was an area recently opened to settlers and I imagined that there might be some opportunities there that could attract me to settle there..

We were to travel to Armidale with other immigrants who wanted to find work somewhere in this developing area. Issell was immediately put to work with another budding Police Supervisor, protecting the two wagons with supplies. Travelling together as a group had become advisable because bushrangers had started to make travel outside Sydney a hazardous affair. Aborigines were not considered a danger to a large travelling group.

As we prepared for the journey I still had the feeling of proceeding into the unknown, not unlike the feelings of leaving Edinburgh. New acquaintances I had made I regarded as friends, for they had opened their hearts to us when we arrived, and in the excitement of the occasion we had responded in like manner. I had made friends at the church and I bid farewell with the understanding that I would keep in touch with them. Issell on the other hand had committed himself to a job that I knew suited him.

The track to Morpeth was an easy part of the journey. The terrain was relatively flat and there were cleared areas where early settlers had removed trees and low level scrub. The scent of Gum trees and bush changed to the pungent smell of smoke in the areas where the settlers burnt piles of removed scrub and trees. The creaking sounds of the wagons as they were drawn by the straining horses whose steel shoes pounding on the track added to the continuously changing sounds. I stored all of these new sensations that were destined to keep changing in the months ahead.

Morpeth is a river port that was used to export the wool clip from the Hunter and New England districts. It also imported supplies for those areas. We added to our heavy load from the local merchant James Taylor. With our load complete we spent our next day travelling to Muscle Brook (Later changed to Muswellbrook). There were no steep hills and the track was maintained so that we arrived in the early afternoon. The wagon master arranged our stay at the Golden Fleece Hotel for reasons only he knew. The hotel was a rowdy establishment generally associated with hotels close to the wharves. The similarities are understandable as it was frequented by the waggoneers who were prone to long drinking sessions during their overnight stopover.

Had we gone only another six miles along the road we might have stayed at the Segenhoe Inn at Aberdeen. Built in 1837, it is a two storey sandstone building claimed to be the finest inn in New South Wales. The Governor had judged it good enough for his accommodation when he ventured into the Hunter river region. I learned that Aberdeen was the home of many Scottish families, and had I allowed the thoughts of home to take control of my mind I would have abandoned this northern adventure for the comfort of a familiar brogue.

After Muscle Brook the road became a series of rocks and holes that challenged the strength of the wagons and bruised our bodies into numb submission. The condition of the road depreciated the further we went, and the areas of cleared land were few and far between. The trees were tall by Scottish standards but not as tall as I have become used to East of Melbourne. The density of the growth between the trees was very heavy and I had to admire the hard work that had been put into clearing a track.

After Tamworth it was no more than an ever widening track, for the drivers sought to avoid the damage caused by previous wagons. There were long slow stretches through hills with rough stony ground where trees and scrub would not grow. The tracks went round the edge of some steep hills and at times the precarious angle of the axels threatened to dump it's load on the ground.

When we camped in the open at night the temperatures fell to uncomfortably low levels, but when the sun came up we could discard our thick outer garments. A hat was a necessity to protect my fair Scottish complexion. It was early spring and the warm day temperatures encouraged indigenous flowers to display their finery to an appreciative new audience from a foreign land.

I had expected to see Aborigines along the way and was not sure what to expect of them. In Sydney the few that ventured into the white man's world walked about as if they owned the place. They may have been entitled to act like this, but it did not go down well with most Sydney people. The wagoners told stories of the primitive way of aboriginal life and they paid little attention to the occasional group that we saw. My casual observation of them was that they were a scruffy lot living in the most basic of shelters, and wearing barely sufficient clothing to cover their bodies. The settlers had lost valuable stock to the aborigines and most had hardened their hearts against them.

At times we came across many acres of burnt out land that had been set alight by the Aborigines. The spring warmth had encouraged the grass to shoot, a bright green against the blackened countryside and contrasting with the dead growths of earlier seasons. This encouraged the kangaroos and wallabies to venture into the open to feed on the fresh green grass. It was then that the Aborigines encircled them and clubbed them to death.

I was starting to see how the conflict between the white settlers and the Aborigines developed into such vicious actions as the Myall Creek Massacre and other lesser actions. Later in my life I learned a lot more about the aborigines and their different tribal customs and spirituality. I came to the conclusion that we would never in my lifetime develop a compromise that would satisfy both the immigrant and the indigenous population.

As we approached Armidale we came upon a family living on the Rocky River, like hermits who sought solitude in a far off land . Samuel McCrossin was an Irishman who had claimed land in the area a year previously and had brought his wife and seven children to live there. He had built a slab hut and was living in the most basic conditions that you could imagine. We stopped to talk with him and I believe that his fierce determination would enable him to continue to exist and develop the fine land that he had chosen.

Finding the property of William Dumaresq created no problems as the road led directly to his property. William's brother, Henry, was private secretary to Governor Darling and it was claimed that the Dumaresq brothers received considerable favours including roads direct to William's properties in Scone and in the New England area. The other brother, Edward, had large pastoral runs in Tasmania, and the family also owned large pastoral runs in the Murray River area. I learnt that the Dumaresq brothers' case was not the only one of this kind. Here was another good lesson to keep in mind; - for success develop the right connections.

The Dumaresq homestead had not had time to become a large pretentious home that some of the pastoralist's homes closer to Sydney had become. It was built beside the Saumarez Creek and the property was called Saumarez. Settlers moving to the less developed country further north relied on the Dumaresq property holding a stock of tools, clothing and basic food.

I spent only a few days at Saumarez, but it was enough for me to gather information about supply to settlements "beyond the boundaries" that I was able to use later in the Gippsland venture. In fact the whole trip north had been a great lesson to me about my new home country. In spite of this I did not feel that New England should be the place where the restless W.B. Howden should settle down.

Issell had met his Police Commissioner and he had been allocated a group of 5 convicts. His days were fully occupied with getting his team together for their ventures into policing the outer reaches of New England. I said goodbye and expressed sincere thanks for his company in the past months. I wished him well and unfortunately we were destined never to meet again. Later I found out that Isell had advanced to the position of Police Magistrate at Armidale. He bought a small property at Uralla, near where we met the Irishman McCrossin on our way north, he married and had a number of children.

For my part I joined the return journey of the two wagons that had brought supplies to Armidale. The sheep shearing season had only just begun and the wagons had only a part load of wool to deliver to the ships at Morpeth. Our party on the return journey was much smaller and the wagons were much lighter loaded with a less valuable cargo for bushrangers. The Waggoners who were full of information about life on the "fringe", and like a dry sponge soaking up water I absorbed their stories and tested out my theories.

In Sydney, I signed off from the merchant who had employed me to accompany his goods to Armidale, and headed back to the same boarding house where I had stayed previously. Issell and I had been sounding boards for each other in the past; now I had only my own head in which to bounce all of my new-found knowledge. The ideas kept swimming round my brain: first my thoughts turned to finding permanent employment with a merchant, then to a boarding house, and for a fleeting moment I considered farm life. Would there be an opening in shipping, certainly not in the police force, but maybe I could retry the family business of jewelry. I could easily establish supply contacts in the jewelry business, but it would take too long, and I had already turned my back on watch making and jewelry long ago.

I set about eliminating the ideas one by one until I came to the conclusion that I should join a merchant, learn their business and eventually be able to branch out on my own. I would not be a shopkeeper type, but an importer of goods distributing to people in some "fringe" area of the colony.

With my mind made up I decided to explore this resolve with the contacts that I had made at Scots church. The Rev.

Lang was particularly helpful. His influence extended far into Australia Felix (as it was then Named) and he had met John Turnbull during one of his visits to Melbourne. John Turnbull had come from Scotland to New Zealand and in 1838 had moved to Melbourne. He was financially well off and John had started a merchant business in Collins St in Melbourne. As Rev. Lang said " He is from good Presbyterian stock" and "I will give you an introductory note if you have a desire to move to Melbourne". I accepted his generous offer and immediately set about finding out more about Australia Felix and in particular Port Phillip District.

I had found the sign post to my future direction, I felt confident in my decision and I stepped out with a world of excitement ahead of me.

Found - My Comfort Zone

In 1803 the Surveyor General of New South Wales, Charles Grimes, rowed 8 miles up the Yarra River to a reef that separated the fresh water from the tidal salt water, He declared this the "most eligible place for a settlement". 32 Years later, in 1835, John Batman landed 500 sheep and 500 cattle at Williamstown. One of his party rowed up the Yarra River to the reef and also declared that would be the place for a settlement

In March 1837 Governor Bourke named the settlement Melbourne. In the presence of about 50 settlers, and at a respectful distance, over 200 Aborigines,. Using William Buckley as interpreter he "exhorted the Aborigines to good conduct and to the missionary George Langhorne". Bourke left behind Robert Hoddle and Robert Russell to map out a plan. The street leading to the reef dividing the fresh from the salt water they named Queen St.

William Buckley escaped custody in 1803 and lived with an Aboriginal mob for the rest of his life. He emerged from their presence at Indented Head in 1835, having lost most of his mother tongue and adopted the Aboriginal tongue. He called the cave at Point Lonsdale, in which he first lived after his escape, his "Sea

Beach Home", and he helped the authorities in their relationship with the Aborigines. *He continued to live the Aboriginal way of life because it gave him "two wives, slaves to attend him and a possum skin rug". He was given a pardon in August 1835.*

By the time that I had taken in what Sydney might have to offer and experimented with New England, it was well into November. The time had not been wasted, for while I had been exploring I had learned as much about myself in those two or three months as I had learned in the preceding twenty three years. I knew that I was now ready to plunge into a career even though my only lead was a letter of introduction to a stranger who had started a merchant business in the recently named town of Melbourne in the Port Phillip District.

I read in the Sydney Herald that Australia Felix south of the Murray River was "a region of flowery plains and green hills". Many settlers had been sold land, although there were complaints that the prices for land grants in this region were considerably higher than land grants in New England. Large numbers of sheep had been shipped into the area west of Melbourne where apparently grazing land was very good. There were articles about cross breeding of sheep that did not interest me, and stories about Charles Francis Latrobe who had been appointed as Superintendent of Port Philip in October and would take up his duties this very month. All of this was of vague interest, like the fact that Latrobe "has a high-pitched voice and effeminate ways and had been tagged with the nickname of "Joey"."

As I scanned the Sydney papers for what little news of Melbourne that I could find, my eyes found a logical attraction to the shipping news. Only a small number of ships went direct to Melbourne, most went via Van Diemen's Land, either Launceston or Hobart. In addition, all of the ships were cargo vessels, some of which took some passengers. The information in the papers was not very helpful so I went to the wharf and secured a passage on a cargo vessel scheduled to sail in a few days and going to Melbourne via Launcestion.

I commenced my second sea voyage with greater maturity gained from the first voyage and life during the most recent two months. And so it was a light heart and a firm resolve that enabled me to enjoy a fast run down the coast of New South Wales, through the Heads and into Port Phillip Bay.

After five days of fair weather sailing the ship berthed at the new Sandridge Pier, later to be called Port Melbourne. From there we were transferred to a lighter to take all passengers and cargo up the Yarra River to Melbourne.

I had no idea where to stay so I set off with my worldly possessions up Queen St to Collins St, where I had been informed by Rev. Lang that the store owned by Mr Turnbull would be found. I came across a small Tavern called the Mitre Tavern in Collins St. I took a room at the tavern for one night and set off to see some of the town before nightfall, having decided to wait until the next day to make acquaintance with Mr Turnbull.

As I stepped out of the Mitre Hotel and looked round I noticed that the two storied Government buildings and hotels were at this end of Collins St. The Government buildings were predictably square boxlike buildings built right to the edge of the pathway with nothing except the squareness to challenge the designer . Pathways had been constructed the length of the street, but the road was unpaved and there was a mixture of stores and houses set behind neat fences as far as I could see. Looking across the road and down the hill I could see a church with long vertical windows and the distinguishing cross on top of the roof.

I set out to see if one of the stores had the name of Turnbull. I did not have to look far to find a store with the name Turnbull Orr and Company proudly displayed on the front of the building. It took only a short time to walk down Collins St, across to Flinders St and back to Queen St. The large building on the banks of the river was the Customs House and other large buildings surrounded the area.

Next morning, after a hearty breakfast at the hotel I strode off confidently to make my acquaintance with Mr Turnbull. When I asked at the office in the front of the building for Mr Turnbull I was surprised to find that there were six Mr Turnbulls. Robert and John were the proprietors of Turnbull Orr and Co, while James, David, George and Patrick had other business interests in Melbourne. The Rev Lang had not indicated that there was more than one Mr Turnbull, but he had mentioned the name of John and I soon found myself sitting in an office with him. From his brogue I knew that he came from Edinburgh, or somewhere in that part of Scotland.

Our conversation soon established that his family came from East Lothian and that he had gone to the Edinburgh High School. I was surprised to find that John was a young man about my own age, in fact only two years older than me. I put my case for requiring a job and in no time I became an employee of Turnbull Orr and Company. The company were in desperate need for someone to improve the process of clearing goods from the ship to the store and to control the increasing amount of paper work created by the shipping companies and the Government Customs House.

While we were talking, Robert Turnbull came into the room and our conversation in broad Edinburgh dialect filled the room and I was able to bring them some news from the Scotland that they had left two years previously. In a short time we had developed a rapport and there was an easy shift to questions about my accommodation in Melbourne. Before I knew it Robert sent out a messenger to a friend who had lodgings and the messenger returned with the news that a room was available at a reasonable rental with all meals as required. The landlord was a member of the Independent church,

St Michael's, situated further along Collins St. It was the only established protestant church at that time, and was the one that I had sighted the day before. That morning, before I had left the company of the Turnbull brothers, I knew that I had advanced from seven months of uncertainty, insecurity and hope and into my comfort Zone.

Learning The Trade

That afternoon I paid off my accommodation at the Mitre Tavern and carried my worldly goods to the home that was to be my long term place of abode. The weatherboard house was in Spring St, a small street at the top of Collins St and therefore only a short walk to the Turnbull and Orr office. My room was small but comfortable and the wife of my landlord insisted on looking after all of my laundry needs. She provided a fine table for breakfast and dinner while I bought my midday meal wherever I was working. She was a very devout Christian lady, full of kindness to everybody and I was indebted to the Turnbulls for the arrangement. The salary I was to receive left me ample money after paying my rent.

Next morning I arrived at the office early and was introduced to some of the people that I would be working with. In particular I was to become involved with clearing the goods and making sure that they arrived in the store in Collins St. From there they would be distributed to the shops in Melbourne and to some of the outlying centres that were springing up throughout the Port Phillip area and beyond.

I wanted to be useful immediately but found that I had a lot to learn about clearing goods from ship to store. Terms such as Bills of Lading, Packing lists and declarations, Invoices and Receipts, consignees addresses and contacts, had to become part of my daily repertoire. I soon found that the customs office was meticulous in the detail required, if the consignor had not filled out the papers correctly they would insist on opening up each package for inspection. By developing shipping and customs contacts I soon learned some "tricks of the trade" and shortcuts that brought company approval.

I really enjoyed the new challenge and I felt that my life had finally taken a direction that would enable me to progress in this new world. Although I felt as if I was on a road that widened to defy perspective, there were days that made the challenge daunting to say the least. The roads in Melbourne were still unpaved except for the road from the cargo wharf, along Queen St and most of Collins St. On other roads, if it rained it was not difficult to have to walk with mud well over your boots or in dry weather the sun was eclipsed by the dust. There was no bridge across the Yarra River and Police Magistrate, Captain William Lonsdale, was severely understaffed of police officers.

The New South Wales Government were extracting large amounts of money from the sale of the fine grazing lands in the district and duty from the sale of liquor and tobacco. They were using this money to improve the infrastructure in the Northern area of New South Wales and an unreasonable amount was transferred to New Zealand to improve the infrastructure there. Because of this the Port Philip District were starved of Government services including the police service.

Melbourne was mostly a migrant community. By contrast Hobart, Launceston, and Sydney were communities in which four fifths of the population were convicts, relatives of convicts or descendants of convicts. By June 1840 the merchants, landholders, stockholders and the working class in Australia Felix were fed up with the way that they were being treated by the northern domiciled Government. They drafted a petition for the separation from New South Wales. It was not until the 5th August 1850 that the act of British Parliament passed the independence of Victoria. It was not until November 11th that people in Victoria could celebrate the fact.

The site of Melbourne was chosen for the availability of fresh water rather than a port and this fact had a direct effect on the problems I was to encounter. Small coastal ships could navigate the bar at the mouth of the Yarra and proceed up the river to the wharf near Queen St. All overseas ships and larger coastal vessels could not navigate the bar. They anchored in Hobson's Bay and were allocated space to unload to lighters at a pier either at Williams Town or Sandridge Pier (Port Melbourne). This created clearing problems so that the average time for the cargo to be cleared was three weeks. I took pride in the fact that in most cases I could beat this time by locating the goods as they were loaded onto lighters and following them through with my good contacts in the Custom House. One of these was the Irishman John Mullaly who had a wonderful way with figures. He eventually became second in charge of the Custom House and then went out on his own as a customs agent. I became friendly with John and was very helpful when I moved to Port Albert.

Clearing of goods was improved considerably in 1840 when Melbourne was declared a free warehousing port. This meant that merchants could hold goods in bonded warehouses and only pay customs duty when goods were sold. This made my job easier and I was able to exploit the system to the advantage of Turnbull, Orr and company.

There were considerable flotsam and Jetsam that drifted down from New South Wales and up from Van Diemen's Land. The unruly activities of this larrikin element reached a crescendo on St Patricks Day in March and the Orangemen celebrating the Battle of the Boyne in July. There were so many arrests that eventually the police Magistrate declared these days as days of drunken debauchery and the police restricted making arrests. It was advisable to keep off the streets on these two days of the year.

There was never a day without excitement and news of interest. The Turnbull boys were constantly observing activity "on the fringe" with the objective of starting a new business venture. Count Strezlecki arrived in Melbourne with glowing descriptions of the area to the east of Melbourne. I could see that it would not be long before John found a new challenge to the east. Strezlecki had set off from Numbla Munji, a cattle property on the Tambo River established by Angus McMillan a year previously. He followed McMillan's trail west and continued on to Melbourne. When he arrived, the Melbourne newspaper blazed his story with vivid descriptions of large areas of fertile land waiting to be developed.

Late in the afternoon John was in the habit of meeting with other businessmen in Melbourne, and their conversation was always about business ventures. The partner in the business, Captain John Orr, was always present and was gung ho on any development prospect. The report by Count Strezlecki set this group into a frenzy, like a gaggle of geese upset by a stranger in it's midst. Here must surely be an opportunity hotter and fresher than the bread from the baker's kitchen in the early morning.

I was often in the office long after the normal business hours and was privileged to be included in these discussions.

It was impossible not to be carried along with the excitement and enthusiasm on this occasion. After two evenings of excited conjecturing and soaring ambition by the business group I went back to Spring St to consolidate my own thoughts. I could become involved if the euphoria of the moment lead to a plan for the future.

McMillan, Strezlecki, the "Clonmel", the "Singapore" and Me from 1841 to 1847

The discovery of Port Albert is linked to each of the above names. Angus McMillan had been moving stock south from Camden for Mr McAlister, a pastoralist of no small means. McMillan had been looking for a route to the sea from McAlister's holding at Numbla Munjei approximately 130 miles north of what is now Port Albert.

Along comes James McArthur who had gathered a party together to establish the likelihood of grazing land between the mountains of Wilson's Promontory and the coast. Governor Gipps had hosted Strezlecki in Sydney and recommended that he satisfy his desire to explore into the southern regions of Australia Felix by joining the McArthur party. The McArthur party proceeded to Numbla Munjie and followed tracks set by McMillan up to the river Riley. From there Strezlecki and Co. struggled on through densely wooded country to the settlement of Western Port. After resting there they proceeded to Melbourne where Count Strezlecki presented a widely published report to Governor Gipps on May 19ᵗʰ 1840.

Angus McMillan continued his efforts to find a route from Numbla Muniei to the coast, and did so on February 14ᵗʰ 1841. He engraved his achievement on a tree at what became the Old Port.

The "Clonmel" was a steamer built in England in 1840 specifically for the Sydney, Melbourne Launceston run. She was on only her second run from Sydney to Melbourne when she was shipwrecked at 3 AM on January 2ⁿᵈ 1841. The crew and 75 passengers were landed with the only casualty, Captain Tollerv who broke an ankle. He organised food and set up camp with guards to protect against aborigines. 5 seamen and 2 passengers set off immediately in a whaleboat and reached the heads to Port Phillip on January 5ᵗʰ. They were towed through the heads and on to Williamstown by the cutter "The Sisters". The "Will Watch" and "The Sisters" returned to rescue the crew and passengers and to recover some of the cargo. By coincidence the survivors camped on the exact place where McMillan made the engraving on the tree 38 days later.

In the days following the trek through Gippsland by McArthur and Count Strezlecki, the "Singapore" was chartered by a syndicate that became the Gipps Land Company Their objective was to find a port and strike inland in the hope of picking up McArthur's tracks and so open a way to the port. They set sail on February the 6ᵗʰ not knowing that McMillan was already blazing a track from Numba Munji.

I had worked diligently for Turnbull Orr and Company and had mastered the ways to clear goods quickly from the wharf and get them into store. The avenues through the annals of government bureaucracy had to be caressed and getting the best out of available carters was an art form that I took pride and satisfaction in mastering.

In return the Turnbull boys accepted me into their family fraternity. During the pioneering days it was common for employers to have a predominance of employees who spoke their own dialect working for them. For similar reasons immigrants drifted into friendship groups of their own kith and kin. I was no exception and found it comforting to be able to spend working time and leisure with the Turnbull boys and the business contacts we made.

Unfortunately work time and leisure time created little opportunity to enjoy social contact with ladies, who were very much in the minority, and in any case were invariably married. The traditions of Scotland however drew us together, and the sound of the bagpipes or the poems of Rabby Burns would stir up the pride within us. Pride for what we had left behind and for the achievements of the substantial number of Scots who had braved the distance and made inroads into this isolated, challenging new world.

Later Angus McMillan was to fall into the same category of kith and kin but now the name that caused all of the excitement was Count Strzelecki. Obviously he was not one of our Presbyterian Brethren but the leader of the exploration, James McArthur, certainly was. Prior to the Count releasing his report James McArthur contacted the Turnbulls and in their conversations revealed a story of their trek from Numbla Munjei through dense forests, swamps and rivers before finally arriving at Westernport and then on to Melbourne. Beside the courage determination and drama of the story there was the element of potential development and land to be exploited. There was no one better in Melbourne town to understand this and have a vision of potential farmland than the Turnbulls. They already had control of large areas of land East of Melbourne.

Captain Orr, in a typically impetuous way, wanted

immediately to lead a group to retrace the path of James McArthur and Strezlecki. More level heads concluded that there must be a better way than to travel overland through dense bushland to the distant fertile area east of the Westernport settlement. It would be easier by sea and it made sense to develop a port for export of stock and import of supplies for the potential community of pioneers who it was assumed would very soon flood into the area. There was one thing certain and that was that John and Robert Turnbull and their friends were determined to exploit the potential rich land that had been recently revealed east of Melbourne. I was in the right place at the right time and from then on I became part of the Turnbull and friends who had the foresight to put their money and energies into a pioneering development in Gippsland.

The question laboured for weeks was exactly where to establish a settlement and when to make the move. Was it better to make the move by sea or send out a party overland. The arguments for each alternative was discussed thoroughly in typical Scottish style, detailing the potential problems associated with each method. Whatever way was chosen it was not going to be an exercise for the faint hearted, and it would have to be financed by a small fortune.

We all knew that McAlister's runs at Numbla Munjie and others in the Omeo area had increasing numbers of stock and that McAlister's manager, Angus McMillan was desperately trying to find an outlet to the sea for export of stock and import of supplies.

There is no doubt that the spark that lit the flame was the arrival at Williamstown of a small party of survivors from the Clonmel. Stories spread through Melbourne like wildfire that the Clonmel had been wrecked on the sands near Corner Inlet at 3 AM on January 2nd. Gales had forced the vessel onto the beach of a long sandspit which is now called Clonmel Island.

While waiting to be rescued, the passengers and crew of the Clonmel inspected the countryside where their wreck landed them. Captain Lewis of "The Sisters" reported in the Port Philip Patriot of "--- a noble inland lake, capricious enough to ride a fleet of shipping secure from every storm, with a navigable passage from Corner Inlet, and also from Shallow Inlet." I admit that comments such as this made the hair on the back of my head stand up as I listened to the visionary comments in the Turnbull and Orr office.

All excuses for lack of action were forgotten. A syndicate was formed and within two weeks Captain Orr placed the following advertisement in the Port Philip Patriot. "Wanted to Charter, a vessel from 80 to 150 tons, apply to Turnbull Orr and Co. 27th of January 1841"

By a stroke of good fortune "The Singapore" was due to arrive from Sydney on January 29th. And it was available for charter. It was immediately engaged for 300 pounds for 3 weeks and 12 pounds per day thereafter. Captain Orr was galvanized into action. He asked me if I would like to help with the venture and sail on "The Singapore " to a port that could be what we were all looking for. I admit that I was swept up by the captain's enthusiasm and accepted immediately, not knowing the hardships that would be involved. The next week was a blur of activity and we could only have achieved what we did because of those hours spent in the Turnbull office meetings since the McArthur and Strezlecki exploration. There was no doubt that the trigger was the "Clonmel" episode.

My job was to organise six months supply of food, tents and some building materials for a small two roomed building. William Brodribb procured agricultural equipment and seeds for planting and hopefully to produce a reliable supply of food. Alexander Kinghorne arranged for eight horses and several cattle, while Captain Orr arranged fire arms which were considered to be necessary to ward off possible attacks from Aborigines. It was hoped that peaceful arrangements could be made with the Aborigines, and for that purpose Robert Turnbull arranged for us to take Charlie Tarra with us. The selection of Charlie had the added advantage that he had been the guide for the Strezlecki and McArthur party and one of the objectives was to strike out from the coast and find the route that they had taken.

The Patriot reporters became aware of our activities and reported on 1/2/1841 "---We alluded in our last number to a project then in embryo for the fitting out of an expedition to Corner Inlet with the view of ascertaining the practicability of communication with Gipps Land from the ocean. We have now the pleasure of informing our readers that a company has been formed under the designation of The Gipps Land Company to set this point at rest, and in the event of a satisfactory solution of the problem to establish a station in some eligible locality, and then endeavour to discover a road by which cattle, Etc. may be conveyed thither from Melbourne. The company have chartered "The Singapore", just arrived from Sydney and taken with them six months supply of provisions, horses Etc.. Messrs Howden, Orr, Rankin, Mcleod, Broadribb, and King proceed in "The Singapore" to Corner Inlet on Wednesday."

Although there were a number of later reports about the Singapore and The Gipps Land Company, this one I kept because it was the first, and I vividly remember how my heart jumped when I read it. This was going to be the pioneering venture that I had been searching for and dreamed of in faraway Scotland. A chance to be a part of opening up real virgin territory. I had no financial claim in the company, my role being to ensure that adequate supplies were assembled and loaded onto the "Singapore". I would then manage the establishment of the store wherever that might be.

A Shambles of Human Endeavour

We did in fact sail on the 6th of February after a hectic rush of organization during the week. The syndicate that now bore the name "The Gipps Land Company" had been submitted by Captain Orr for the Governors approval. It would be months before the company approval came through due to the poor communications between Sydney and Melbourne. The newspapers never did get all of the names involved in the Gipps Land Company right, and it was of no consequence because the interested parties changed before the authority from the Governor arrived. By that time some of the members had decided not to go ahead and within a year the name of the company had been changed to "The Port Albert Company" with a different group of partners.

As we left Williamstown dock the company details were far from my thoughts. By chance I had become part of an exciting new adventure and I was going to make the most of it. There was a hot north wind that took us quickly out to the heads of Port Philip Bay, the ship was reacting to counter currents of the changing tide at the heads and I stood on the deck with the inspiring character, Captain Orr. The spray was splashing our faces as I turned to him and said "John, my heart tells me that we are starting on a successful and satisfying venture". The words were out before I thought of what I had said. Until then I had always addressed him as "Captain Orr" or just "Captain". In hindsight this was a realisation that I had been accepted into the company of investors as an equal. I had no money in the company but I had invested a lot of energy into the Turnbull and Orr Company in Melbourne and they had given me the responsibility of organising the stores for the Gipps Land venture. I knew that my efforts for the company were appreciated.

It took just two days to arrive at Corner Inlet but we wasted two weeks of good charter time unsuccessfully exploring for the "—noble inland lake, capricious enough to ride a fleet of shipping safe from any storm." reported by Captain Lewis. Frustrated, we sailed back to the site of the Clonmel wreck and proceeded to unload the provisions on the east side of the stream that was later named the Albert River.

Some of our party erected tents and slept on shore while the others stayed on board. While the tents were being erected several Aborigines appeared and began to make off with some of the stores. They were driven off by the Captain and some of the others who had loaded their guns with gunpowder only. John Orr had also taken the precaution of bringing a cannon for protection and when fired a few times was sufficient to deter the inquisitive natives. We later placated them with some gifts to show our desire for peace. Although Charlie Tarra could not speak their language they could see that one of their kind was not harmed by the strange invaders of their territory.

It was now late February and we were unaware that while we were exploring the area by sea, Angus McMillan had reached the ocean on February 14th very close to where we decided to settle and where the Clonmel passengers had camped. McMillan had left his message blazed on a tree to prove the date of his overland arrival there. Without that there would always have been questions about his claims.

Unloading our cargo from The Singapore was not an easy task. We could not anchor close to shore and had to sling the load first onto smaller vessels and ferry it to shore. This was routine for most of the cargo but the animals had to be slung from the Singapore into the water, a rope was tied round their horns or neck and they swam and were pulled to shore before being taken to a hastily erected fenced area. The operation took all day and was completed with the loss of only one bullock that managed to free itself from the sling and was drowned. After butchering, it provided hearty meals of fresh meat for the next few days. On one evening, after a long hard day of labour and a good meal washed down with ample liquor, we decided that Albert Town was an appropriate name for our little settlement of fenced cattle, a store and tents. It was a wonderful moment of camaraderie that we could recall during the unexpected difficulties that we were to encounter during the years ahead. In the euphoria of the moment, the river on which we camped was called Prince Albert River after the Prince Consort. West of this was another river that by popular vote was named the Tarra River after our aboriginal guide Charlie Tarra.

Building the store became a priority because pilfering by the Aborigines continued in spite of our guns, Charlie Tarra's persuasion and plying them with gifts. John Orr reminded us that our objectives were not only to establish a settlement, but also to find a land route back to Melbourne. We had also to check if there were any of the Turnbull and Orr company goods, or anything else on the Clonmel that could be salvaged.

While some of the group made the settlement ready for those who would stay behind, others explored beyond the camp area with the help of Charlie Tarra. Their hope was to find the route taken by James McArthur and Strezlecki.

28 days after arriving in the area I returned on the "Singapore" for Melbourne, leaving Charlie Tarra and a small group to return overland . A superintendent and 3 others were to stay on, having 5 months supply of provisions, horses and cattle. Our excitement about the prospects were still sky high.

The land group arrived in Melbourne about 4 weeks after the "Singapore". By this time John Orr had already lodged application on behalf of the Gipps Land Company to exploit the "Special Survey" arrangement made by Superintendent Latrobe. Orr had mapped out 5120 acres of land between the Prince Albert River and the Tarra Rivers which he planned to sub divide and make a lot of money for the Gipps Land Company. Unfortunately for Turnbull and Orr, Governor Gipps had other ideas and overruled the special survey rules of Latrobe, insisting that a detailed survey would be conducted, and that the Government would have first choice of land and control the sale of land from Sydney, the proceeds of which had to be paid into the NSW Government coffers. This New South Wales and London intervention was a bone of contention with all of us in the southern area of Australia Felix, and it was not until 1853 that the newly formed state of Victoria got independent control over land. We could never understand why when the British Parliament declared Victoria, Tasmania and South Australia independent states, the government of NSW continued their control for another four years.

The Gipps Land Company did not get the land that John Orr had asked for, but six months later they did get the same area of

5120 acres north of the area that the Government surveyor had mapped out for a town.

Back in Melbourne I continued my responsibilities with Turnbull Orr and Company including the extra responsibility to ensure that the party remaining at Port Albert had adequate supplies and to cater for the needs of the Gipps Land Company.

To start with, the settlement remained at the mouth of the Albert River and was basically a group of tents on the beach, with the store the only substantial building. The land behind the beach had low scrub and wetland, and as you progressed inland there were high gum tree forests. As time went on settlers arrived to take advantage of the grazing land being created inland from Port Albert. It sounds easy now but tree felling and scrub clearing caused many a calloused hand and broken back.

Our store beside the Albert river and the area around it was nothing to be proud of. There was no order in the way the tents and a few wooden houses were set out. Water was conveniently available from the river but a small number of deep pits were all that was available for sewerage. Other waste was carelessly scattered round the fringe of the settlement.

The Turnbull and Orr Company continued to ship supplies that were sold from the store by the superintendent at the time. They chartered ships that traded from Melbourne to Hobart, Launceston, Adelaide and now to Port Albert. They later had ships of their own. Cash was not always exchanged for goods, but promissory notes and articles were traded and if appropriate offers of labour were accepted. Our company had most of the growing business but there were other small traders who recognised the potential and moved into the area. To be truthful the first nine months on the banks of the Albert were very frustrating. Unloading ships from well offshore onto sand and mud that became badly cut up by cart wheels and the horses hooves was no fun. When it came to loading cattle onto the ships it became chaotic. First the cattle had a rope from the ship tied round their horns and were coaxed into the water amid much bellowing from the cattle and shouting from the cattle drovers. The poor beasts were compelled to swim out to the ship by energetic crew pulling on the rope. When they reached the ship a sling was fastened round them and they were hoisted on board.

It was not long before a more convenient place to load and unload was found and that was at the narrow spit of land where the Tarra River met the sea. There was greater depth here that allowed the ships to come closer to shore and this spit of land became known as Shipping Point.

As I write this it seems that there was suddenly much activity at Port Albert, however, in the first six or nine months this was not the case. What activity there was could only be described as disorganised and crude. The people who had decided to live there also deserved the same description, disorganised and crude. Some of the investors in The Gippsland Company became disillusioned and withdrew, leaving those left to replace it with The Port Albert Company, dominated by John and Robert Turnbull and John Orr. The new company expected to take control of Shipping Point as their rite but they were prevented from doing so by the Government surveyors who chose Shipping Point and surrounds as the site for the town of Port Albert. Not to be outdone The Port Albert Company later bought some of the land at Shipping point from the Government from which they were able to control trade. Control it they certainly did, with Robert being the dominant member of the family in Port Albert.

Streets were yet to be established but were laid out in the plans and the land designated as the town of Port Albert was subdivided. The place that we had established from the original landing of the "Singapore" became known as the Old Port. With Turnbull Orr and Company dominating the trade in and out of the port it became necessary to build a substantial store on the new town site. It was into this situation that I came permanently to Port Albert to improve the trade through Port Albert for the Port Albert Company. There were probably about 15 people living at the port and the settlement at Tarraville had about twice that number with Alberton the same number as Tarraville.

During the first few years I lived and worked in Port Albert, my only contact with the other settlements was with the small shops and traders. Each settlement had its own character shaped by the people that settled there. Alberton was a particularly unsavory place, infested with villains from Hobart who committed crime without fear and then disappeared into the bush. Tarraville was a rather miserable little place with two stores to supply the cattlemen who came down with the stock and yarded them there waiting for the arrival of a ship. With much spare time they spent a lot of it in the hotel with the consequence that there was plenty of drunken revelry while they were in town. The population of Old Port did not have to wait for the cattlemen to consume the liquor, the locals were well practiced and I preferred to visit there only during daylight.

With the number of Scottish Families taking up settlement in the hinterland of Port Albert you could have been excused for thinking that The Lord had picked up part of Scotland and placed it in Gippsland. The first of these was Lachlan Macalister who employed Angus McMillan. There were also the Macfarlane's, the Buckley and the Bayliss families and a host of Scottish Macs, all who used the Port Albert Company for supplies and shipping their cattle. The largest and unexpected settler was the Laird of Glengarry, Aneas McDonald. He came on the scene about the same time as myself and brought with him a prefabricated home for the family. The home and other buildings were assembled at "Greenmount" where the laird, and 23 staff intended setting up a dairy farm. After six months he tired of this, sold everything and moved to Sydney. The home became the public house at Old Port for a time before it was transferred again to Port Albert where it became the basis for the Port Albert Hotel that I managed and held the licence.

During the day life was busy, there was not time to think about anything but the business of Turnbull and Orr who were interested in anything to make some money. In the evening however I sometimes thought "why in the name of Scotland was I in this out of the way place, removed from family, without a wife or any prospect of finding one in this male dominated dump". Alberton in particular became a dump for the "scum" of Australia Felix. Escaped convicts and their friends congregated there and the criminal element and the aborigines targeted the store on a regular basis. It became unprofitable to run a store there and we packed up the Turnbull and Orr store and concentrated on the Port Albert and Tarraville stores which were more in line with the flow of traffic between Shipping Point and the settlers who were increasing in numbers in the hinterland. When the store was removed from Alberton the settlement faded away, as did the criminal element.

It was in the middle of the first winter that the Glengarry store was moved to Port Albert to serve as a hotel, and the next year Robert Turnbull, who spent a lot of his time at the Port, bought it and asked me to manage it. The building that had been designed as a house required a lot of work to make it more practical as a hotel, and skilled carpenters were not readily available. Supervising the extensions and upgrading the rooms consumed a large part of my daily activity which I found very satisfying. It came at a time when I needed a project that took me away from some of the inconvenient and improper activities in the settlement. Water still had to be carted from the Old Port and the roads in town were either avenues of mud or clouds of dust. Supplies by ship from Port Phillip and Sydney were made on a very irregular schedule and the overland route to Port Philip had not yet been established. The bullock carts carrying building materials and goods to Alberton and Tarraville would become bogged after rain. To travel beyond these settlements you had to choose a track that you hoped would lead to your desired destination. Crime and drunken carousing continued uncontrolled, particularly in the Old Port district.

Promotional sign at modern Port Albert

*Port Albert Hotel Today is basically the same as when
W.B. held the licence from 1844 to 1851. Turnbull
and Howden continued ownership until 1856*

**The Turnbull and Orr Warehouse 1844. Most goods into Port Albert
were stored here during the first years of the existence of Port Albert.**

Settlers who had brought their cattle down from the north
were anxious to find a reliable overland route to Port Philip

and a number of attempts ended in disaster with the loss of hundreds of cattle. The drovers who brought their cattle for shipping from Port Albert to Hobart and New Zealand told some harrowing stories about driving cattle through dense bush, and crossing swamps and rivers in their attempts to reach the Port Philip markets. After spending weeks trying to get through they were often forced to live on the meat of Koalas because they were easy to catch or shoot. Eventually an overland route was temporarily abandoned and sea transport was the only route for a number of years.

9

Same Place – New Direction

It was not through lack of desire and serious thought that I had not found a wife with whom I could share the highs and lows of Port Albert living. The time to act on my desires came however with the hotel project. I was in my late twenties, I had experienced life in New South Wales and in Melbourne, and most recently I had been intimately involved with the establishment of a new settlement that had the potential of becoming a legitimate competitor with Port Philip. The hotel was somewhere that I could invite a wife to live, in spite of the chaos and uncertainty that surrounded us. It was therefore with a positive state of mind that I sailed back to Melbourne once more on one of the Turnbull chartered ships.

In the two or three years that I had spent at Port Albert, the Turnbulls in Melbourne had gathered an increasing number of Scottish families into their social circle. Into this scene I launched myself with a new incentive to find a wife. I had established a sound career with the Turnbull and Orr company and I now appreciated the discipline invoked by my parents to always act as a gentleman. I felt confident that I could correctly approach a young lady and I knew that I had some stability to offer a potential life partner. There certainly was not a big field of young ladies to project my new found confidence and determination. When I mentioned Port Albert, the reaction of the young ladies, who had settled into life in Melbourne, was that Port Albert was miles away from civilisation in an unchartered jungle. Unfortunately, those who had visited Port Albert related only the stories that would create interest through sensation, and these were invariably the dark side of the settlement designed to shock their audience. The reputation of Port Albert in Melbourne therefore was not good. My strategy changed from finding an immediate life partner, to persuading a potential wife to visit Port Albert as my guest in the hotel, with the hope of showing them the good side of the Port. Kathleen was a young lady who was prepared to speculate when I outlined my plan. In order to avoid any unwanted approach from other men, my chosen adventurer and I embarked on a return passage to Port Albert as Mr. and Mrs. Howden.

Kathleen and I maintained the "Married" cover for a few weeks but eventually it had to be uncovered as we slept in different rooms. The whole area, including Tarraville, Alberton, and other outlying settlements were known as Port Albert. The total population was 120 of which 49 were convicts. Of the 25 people in the town of Port Albert 17 were men with six women and two children, a statistic that Kathleen was soon to find out and dislike. At the time most of the other women were attached to the less savoury male residents. She was not inclined to develop social contact with these ladies and my carefully laid strategy to woo a wife was shattered by the dismal social life at the time.

The strategy was not helped by a rumor that a white lady had been captured by the Aborigines and held captive in one of the Aboriginal communities outside Tarraville. The captive was reputed to be a Scottish Highlander and search parties were formed to attempt to rescue her. She was never found and it was realized, some months later, that the female capture story originated when a group of Aborigines stole the figurehead of a voluptuous lady from a wrecked ship. Unfortunately, Kathleen had already departed when the source of the rumour was revealed.

Before she left Kathleen experienced some innocent excitement at Port Albert that would enable her to relate the light side of the Port life on her return to Melbourne. The ship on which she would return to Melbourne came from Hobart carrying an elephant for the Martin brothers living on a run at Alberton. Where the elephant came from originally nobody knows, but the Martins planned to use it to clear the scrub on their property. When the word circulated that an elephant had arrived on a ship and was to be unloaded at the port the whole town was there to observe the spectacle; and spectacle it was. The process of loading cattle from shore to ship and then winching them on board in a sling might have been practical in reverse if the elephant did not weigh more than twice that of the fattest bullock. The sling was fitted to the elephant with the expectation of lifting the trumpeting animal, slinging it out from the ship and lowering it into the water. When the winch attempted to take up the weight the elephant became unbalanced and toppled onto its side amidst much trumpeting and amusement from the gathered audience. In trying to lift the elephant back onto its feet, the winch, designed for much lighter cattle, was no match for the weight of the elephant. The only means of getting the beast into the water was to push it overboard. The crew soon found that when an elephant decides that he is not going to be pushed off his feet into the unknown he can make it very difficult for mere men. The crew called for help from the substantial number of bystanders. With the sound of shouting and trumpeting the hapless elephant was launched off the side of the ship in a most ungainly entry into the water.

On shore, there was speculation from the onlookers about whether an elephant could swim. Swim it did, but it wanted to swim in any direction away from ship and man. Rowing boats put out to prod and finally coerce the new farm animal to shore where it stood, making a noisy protest, until its owners finally worked out how to lead it off to its new home.

I was very glad for this diversion at the time although I still felt sad as I took Kathleen out onto the ship that would take her back to Melbourne. She was a fine lass and under different circumstances we might have found happiness together. In two days she would be back among her Melbourne friends and I would continue with the challenge before me and with a determination not to give up the quest to find a wife.

The elephant proved to be a bad investment for the Martin boys. It did not achieve the objective of clearing the scrub from their property. It did scare the aboriginal labourers away and finally wandered away to die many miles away in the Australian bush.

Unlike the debacle of the elephant, the Turnbull and Orr company was growing daily and they had a hand in many developments in the greater Port Albert. I was involved either directly or indirectly with most of it. Goods exported through the port were increasing as the locals found new ways of subsidising existing businesses and farms. Tannin from the tea tree bark had become a profitable side line for many settlers who were satisfying the demand for tannin in tanning of hides. It was also an important ingredient in the treatment of the ever increasing number of boilers on shore and on the sea. Sheep became a very profitable business, but not only for the settlers who were bringing more sheep down from New South Wales. The wool was exported through Port Albert and it was not long before Turnbull and Orr started a meat processing works. The next logical step was a tallow factory where the hindquarters of sheep were retained for the meat but the forequarters were more valuable when rendered down as tallow. The skins were treated in the tanning factory and so developed a valuable industry based on the sheep that benefitted the farmers, the labourers and the Turnbull family who were all able to improve their income.

With the increase of trade out and into the port, a need for customs control developed and it fell on me to use the knowledge I had accumulated working with Turnbull and Orr in Melbourne to establish the custom house. Life at Port Albert was becoming much better organised and my life was definitely moving in the right direction. Robert Turnbull spent a lot of his time and energies at Port Albert and he offered me a partnership in a new company to be called Turnbull and Howden. This company embraced some of the developing enterprises in the district.

Living in the hotel had advantages and disadvantages. It was impossible to avoid becoming involved in any unpleasantness between guests. On the other hand, I was kept abreast with all of the activity in the greater Port Albert and beyond, and this was helpful in conducting other branches of our business. There was plenty of illegal liquor being brewed and this was inevitably the source of some of the unpleasantness that I sometimes had to sort out, there being no police or any other sense of law and order. This changed two or three years later with the arrival of Charles Tyers as Commissioner for Crown

Lands. His responsibility was to establish law and order, record the boundaries of runs, the sites of roads and townships, collect fees and generally carry out the business of Government.

One of Tyers earliest successes was to gain control of the deteriorating relationship between the Aborigines and the settlers. Conflict was bound to happen as the settlers transgressed the traditional lands of the Aborigines and the Aborigines helped themselves to the new fat "game" that the settlers "provided". They liked to possess many of the "luxuries" brought by us foreigners and believed that the goods belonged equally to them. The reaction of the white people varied considerably. The best of them made friends with the Aborigines and some trained them to work on the farms. Others reacted to Aborigines spearing their cattle by forming retaliatory groups to track down the offenders and kill them. Angus Macmillan told me that there were extreme cases where indiscriminate killing of Aborigines took place involving the death of innocent women and children. Angus was very considerate to the Aborigines but he was aware that a group of his stockmen had been guilty of indiscriminate killing. Such occurrences were kept quiet because of the likely hanging of the offenders, and it is possible that all together there were up to 400 deaths of Aboriginals and only a small number of white deaths in retaliation before Tyers arrived on the scene.

Another of Charles Tyers successes was to control the excessive drinking of alcohol. Illicit stills and sly grog shops had sprung up and the strength and quantity of alcohol was out of control. Our hotel did not have a liquor license, in fact I bought some land and started a soft drink factory which I owned for a few years before selling it. We eventually obtained a license to brew beer, and this enabled us to control the strength of the liquor being consumed by our customers. When I applied for a liquor license for the Port Albert and the Tarraville hotel I was able to exert some control by selling only our own beer.

For a short time management of the hotel and it's refurbishment gave me a focus and little time for anything else. As other business interests came into the Turnbull and Howden fold I handed over much of the running of the hotel to others. I bought a cottage in Victoria St that enabled me to live apart from hotel life, but living in a house on my own strengthened the desire to find a partner.

Contact with "home" in Scotland was significantly improved with the establishment of a regular pack horse route to Melbourne and a post office at Port Albert. A letter from home announced that my sister Ann had become engaged to be married to Rev. Login in the Orkney Islands. At that time I was thirty, I had my own house, a growing business and a young sister who by the time that I received that letter, could already be married. The arrival of the letter from home marked a new resolve to find a wife.

The next week I was due for another visit to Melbourne. As often happened when in Melbourne I went with James Buchanan to the Melbourne post office to pick up the mail. Even though the arrival of my personal mail never coincided with these visits, it did give me that feeling that there was a line of communication to family. On one of these visits we met Sarah Leage, who was also picking up her mail, and in the course of conversation it was established that she was unattached. Turnbull and Orr and the company had arranged a social evening for that day. Thinking of my interest he invited Sarah to the evening and the invitation was accepted with enthusiasm. During the evening the other guests made sure that we had plenty of time to talk together. I told Sarah about Port Albert and my involvement there. She told me that she had been in

Melbourne for seven years and had been married to James Leage but they had drifted apart. Sarah and her sister, Hannah, had arrived on the "Westminster" in company of a number of other young ladies. Apparently the arrival in Melbourne was an unnerving experience as a large number of the single male population were at the wharf hoping to find a partner. The fact was that within two weeks both Hannah and Sarah had found a partner and were married. For Hannah it had turned out to be a satisfactory marriage and she already had four children, the number of children later growing to nine. For Sarah the situation was not so happy. Sarah was able to read and write which had given her confidence to leave her husband and to find work. This enabled her to stay in Melbourne living with her sister. Hannah could neither read nor write so that it was fortunate that their marriage had been a success.

During that Melbourne visit, Sarah and I met each day and when it was time to return to Port Albert it was with a promise to meet again on my next visit to Melbourne. I was in no hurry to repeat my last attempt to attract a wife to Port Albert even though my lot had vastly improved and the area was much more settled and law abiding than four years ago.

When we did meet again we were both ready for a proposal from me and acceptance from Sarah. It was not a surprise to anyone so we hastily arranged with the Presbyterian minister Rev James Forbes. He was agreeable to the marriage for I had attended his church when I was in Melbourne with quite a few of the staff at Turnbull and Orr. Sarah was not a member of the Presbyterian Church, which was duly recorded on the marriage certificate, and it was considered advisable that she use her maiden name of Sarah Cooper and sign the marriage certificate as a spinster. That way the minister and the Presbyterian Church of Scotland could smile upon the marriage.

I chose James Buchanan as my best man and Sarah asked her good friend from Geelong, Ellen Whitmore, to be her bridesmaid. Most of the staff of Turnbull and Orr attended the wedding and Hannah and her family, along with friends on both sides, enjoyed a very happy occasion. John Turnbull was master of ceremonies at the reception that turned out to be a major social event with our friends at Turnbull and Orr.

Two days later we were on a ship to Port Albert, legally wed as Mr and Mrs Howden. The greeting at the Port was as joyous as the celebration in Melbourne. It was an excuse to have a party at the hotel with my friends, and an opportunity to introduce Sarah to people, who I hoped would become her friends in future.

We lived in the house in Victoria St, and Sarah, who was a good cook and kept a tidy home for us both, was making good progress with friendships in the area. An unfortunate triplet of circumstances upset the applecart and greatly unsettled Sarah. It was just one month after we arrived back in Port Albert when Thomas Ritchie was found with his skull crushed in and his throat cut, lying with his dog, also brutally killed, in a paddock opposite Neilson's Royal Hotel in Alberton. The most likely culprits were a drunken group who left the hotel with him the night before, but John "Pretty Boy" Healy was chosen as the guilty one and was taken into custody. There being no facility for a trial in the Port area, he had to be held in custody for about three months before a ship was available to take him to Melbourne for trial. During this time the "debate" in all of the hotel bars in the district centred on whether Healy was guilty, and if not him, who committed the brutal crime. The debate of course overflowed into the whole community and people felt threatened because there was no secure place for Healy to be held. They knew that the police force was undermanned and that there was a section of the community who wanted him released. He did face trial in Melbourne, found guilty and was hung; but the mood of the community at the time unsettled Sarah.

Not long after this incident a shipload of convicts from Hobart was landed at Port Albert and taken to Alberton where they did not take long to riot. The fighting and looting continued for at least a week before some order was restored by Commissioner Tyers and a police force inadequate for such a dangerous situation. In the towns we questioned the need to import convicts to satisfy labouring needs of the settlers. The settlers of course wanted all of the labour they could get to clear the trees on their runs.

The coup de grace for Sarah was closer to home. There was a major theft from our own hotel from where a number of valuable items were stolen. The culprit was never found and a disturbed Sarah put her arms round me one evening and pleaded to go back to stay with her sister until life was more settled at Port Albert. In fairness I could not refuse and arrangements were made for her to leave on the next ship returning to Melbourne. We parted on the wharf at Port Albert with both of us expecting this to be only a temporary separation, knowing that I would be visiting Melbourne regularly and expecting that all would be well in the long run.

The Golden Years

The 1850's and 60's were certainly the golden years for Gippsland and Port Albert. Cattle exports picked up after the slowdown of the late 1840's. There was a change from predominantly sheep to predominantly cattle, and the agricultural diversification developed. Wheat, barley, fruit, including oranges and grapes, potatoes and vegetables were produced and marketed. From 1845 to 1859 the area under crop increased from 106ha. to 1426 ha. and the number of holdings from 71 to 224, all this within the Alberton district that had a total area of 6,732 ha.. There was still no reliable land route to Melbourne so that the port and shipping was the lifeline for the area, and this was controlled by the Turnbull connections of which one W.B. Howden was to have a progressively greater influence and financial interest.

It was outside Alberton that the greatest influence occurred. Gold was found at Omeo in 1851, followed by Crooked River, Boggy Creek and Walhalla. More gold was taken out of these fields than the total of Ballarat and Bendigo combined. The Turnbull and Howden Company controlled the shipment of gold and the movement of people and supplies in and out of Gippsland through ownership of the land, warehouses and hotel on the only wharf in Gippsland. They acted as agents for most of the shipping companies.

In the wider world the industrial revolution gained exponential pace. Petroleum was distilled for the first time which opened the door for a commercially successful internal combustion engine. Battles between pro slavery and "free state" settlers in America directly precipitated the Civil War. Charles Darwin published "the Origin of the Species" and Queen Victoria's first grandchild was born in 1859. The Queen's husband bought land in Scotland on which Balmoral Castle was built and completed in 1855. The Crimean War 1854-56 was fought between Russia and the UK, France, Sardinia and the Ottoman Empire.

After saying goodbye to Sarah I walked slowly back to the Hotel. At no time had I considered moving back to Melbourne but I had a strange mixture of guilt, depression and remorse. I was confident then that I could make a success out of life at Port Albert and I had tried to convince Sarah that my dreams could be realised and there would be a life for us both here. It is easy to say now that I should have understood Sarah better and realised that she would compare her situation with that of her sister Hannah. At the time Melbourne offered her a much more comfortable life than Port Albert but I was determined to convert the foothold that I had established in Port Albert into the vision I brought with me from Scotland.

When I sat down in my office at the hotel my mind was in turmoil. It was late April, just one month since I brought Sarah to Port Albert. There was a cold wind outside and rain was starting to beat on the window, if it kept up, the mud on the road would be deep enough to cover my boots. I was in no mood for any serious thinking so I gathered my coat, shouting to the barman that I would see him in the morning and headed toward Victoria St.

On the way out the door Davey Fermaner invited me for a drink, which was declined abruptly. I immediately regretted this reply because our trade through the port relied on the skills of Davey to pilot the ships through the changing channels and sandbars. As I was carried by a cold tail wind and rain down the street, two aboriginals battled the head wind wrapped in government issued blankets that were a poor substitute for the possum skin rugs that usually covered their skinny frames against the cold.

At home I surveyed the place that had given me only a short introduction to married life. My gaze fell on the letters that had come from home on the ship that took Sarah back to Melbourne. I had read these only briefly, so I sat down and allowed the written words to take my mind back to the family that I loved and needed to help me unburden my mind. Father wrote about the business and the changes in lifestyle that troubled him, but the two letters that interested me most were one from sister Ann and one from brother Andrew. Ann was married now and both showed more than a casual interest in the lifestyle in Australia Felix. After drowning myself in the love and concern in these letters my mood changed and I sat down at my desk at home to tell them, not so much about the state of my recent marriage, but about the prospects that were emerging out here in Gippsland.

I had put a claim deposit on a plot of land at "Green Hills" between Alberton and Tarraville and I had plans for building a house on the property. I owned a house in Victoria St that I called home, and business opportunities were presenting themselves regularly. Managing the hotel provided a stable source of income and I had hopes of becoming a part owner with Robert Turnbull. The diversion of writing letters to home lifted my spirit and I was more convinced than ever that my future lay in Port Albert.

In future letters I wrote about the bright future initiated by the discovery of gold and the strategic importance of Port Albert in the development of Gippsland. It was generally six months between writing each letter and receiving a reply but I sensed that Ann and her husband William Spence Login showed interest in coming to Australia. Spence was a Presbyterian Minister from the Orkney Islands and I emphasised the considerably warmer climate and the beautiful Spring and Autumn days here. I was careful not to explain that the toilet and waste product dump was a deep pit in the back yard over which was constructed a respectable but small building. I would leave it for them to find when they arrived that for their water supply they had to rely on tanks beside the house that filled with water from the roof. They would become aware during a dry period that a horse drawn water-tank with contents of dubious quality bore water from Tarraville would fill their house tank. These facts and the terror of droughts, fire and floods could be much better explained after they arrived.

The need for a Presbyterian minister in the area was the subject of the last letter before Spence asked me to investigate the chance of getting an appointment in Gippsland. I found out that a vacancy had been declared at Flooding Creek (later Sale) and Spence lost no time in applying to fill the new position that would include an area as large as Scotland that he would have to travel to tend his parishioners. The appointment was made from Scotland and the authorities there had no knowledge that there were no roads as they knew them in his huge parish. Spence was in for a shock but his training period in Sydney and Melbourne would soften the blow.

Youngest Sister, Janet, had also married a minister on the Orkney Islands, the Rev. George Traill, and they were obviously impressed by my glowing reports. The girls were living near one another and Ann now had four children and Janet had one. I imagined their talk about bringing up the babies and how they must have talked about living in this new country. I was delighted when Janet wrote to say that she was coming with George and Mary.

Ann, Spence and the children arrived first in August 1853 and stayed in Sydney and Melbourne for almost a year before transferring to the Gippsland parish centred in Sale. Janet, George and young Mary arrived in October 1853 .

Janet was only 16 years old and Ann was 21 when I left Scotland fourteen years ago, and at the time I did not expect to see them again. I knew that their three months at sea with children would be challenging and potentially dangerous, so I was determined to meet them when they arrived. Ann was due to arrive in Sydney and my arrival by ship from Port Albert was a few days earlier. There were not many of the congregation left that I knew at Scots Church in Sydney fourteen years ago, but those who were there were able to direct me to the authorities in the church who would be responsible for Spence and his family when they arrived. I found out where they would be staying and made sure that the essential things would be there for them when they arrived. A fly swat was high on the list, some fruit and soft drinks for the children and flowers for Ann. I also bought Ann the most fashionable broad brimmed hat that I could find, and hats for Spence and the children. I did not want them to experience the sunburn that I had to endure in Sydney even though it was the middle of winter when they arrived. I set the hats out on the beds and the flowers and soft drinks appropriately positioned; the next day was going to be the happiest day of my life.

I stayed in a hotel close by and I was awake with excitement most of the night. My actions I admit were very childlike as I walked to the wharf to find out where and when the ship would dock. When it arrived, Ann, Spence and the children were waving from the deck and I knew that they would be feeling very relieved that their time at sea was at an end, at least until their next trip south. They all experienced the "funny" sea legs but they definitely appreciated the fresh water and food that was available. That night I sat with my sister, her husband and three children to a sumptuous meal together. Questions and answers flew as we tried to bridge the 14 years of separation and the different directions that we had taken. Ann was no longer the sister who helped father manage the family back in Edinburgh. She was very definitely a mother of her own children and wife of a minister of religion with responsibilities to both. Through all of the excitement it was clear that although Ann would always be my sister, her primary responsibilities had changed.

We had another two days together before my ship left for Port Albert where there was an abundance of activity as the rush for gold gathered pace. The days with Ann, Spence and the children prepared me for the reunion with Janet and her family. I learned that I should handle that differently.

It was only two months before Janet would arrive in Melbourne. It was two months of power activity as Shipping Point became a hive of activity with gold prospectors arriving almost daily and goods exported and imported to service the sharply increased population and growth in industry. As I busied myself with the increased trading my mind kept revisiting the meeting with Ann's family. Of greatest concern was the news about my father. He was now aged sixty six and he lived with Andrew in the same home that I left. Three of his four surviving children were now committed to living in a country three months away in travel time and communication. He had been the sole parent since my mother died during the birth of Janet, and now, after the double responsibility of breadwinner and homemaker, he was left with one unmarried son at home. I also felt sorry for Andrew, who probably felt a responsibility to stay with father. Maybe Janet would have some positive thoughts.

I met Janet, George and Mary when the good ship "London" arrived in Melbourne in October. I had arranged to be in Melbourne for some business commitments so my mood was different to when I met Ann. In addition, Janet and her family were to come back to Port Albert with me and we would have more time to talk about the family.

We stayed only one night in Melbourne before sailing to Port Albert. This was not long enough for the Traills to get their land legs but it did allow them to meet my colleagues at Turnbull and Orr who had been my family for about twelve years. It was such a wonderful feeling introducing them and they were so well received by everyone who were eager to hear news from "Home". That one night in Melbourne was shared with my extended family and they all doted on young Mary who performed beautifully for her mother with the sweetest of Scottish brogues. It made our Scottish staff feel homesick.

The voyage back to Port was a very pleasant two days. The sailing weather was perfect, but of greater importance was the enthusiasm that Janet and George displayed to everything we discussed. The rapport was from the heart and I knew that our future relationship would be bright.

On our arrival, I settled the Traills in at the Tarra Vale Hotel where I had the licence at the time. I had relinquished the licence at the Port Albert Hotel and although we still owned it, the atmosphere there was related to the trading activity surrounding the wharf. I would have liked to have put them up at Green Hills where I had already finished building one house, but It was already rented out to Dr Hedley and his wife. I had plans to build another house set separately on the high ground behind the existing house.

Next day was the most joyous day that I had spent since my arrival in Australia. I arrived at the hotel mid-morning with the best Jinker in the area and we drove from Tarraville down to Port Albert. Mary and I were now good friends, and when we alighted I hoisted her on my shoulders and I paraded her with her mother and father first to the Port Albert hotel and then to the store, the warehouse and the bond store. I was so proud to introduce them to friends and colleagues. As we walked past the cattle yard on the wharf Mary excitedly squealed "look Coos".

As we approached we met Angus McMillan who regularly brought down cattle for export to Tasmania and New Zealand. Angus was one of the members of our Scottish "family" in Gippsland and he often stayed at the Port Albert Hotel. he purchased his household requirements from our store.

Mary's "what's that" and "look" did have some embarrassing moments as she pointed at Aborigines and Chinese walking down the street. By now mixed races in Port Albert had become an accepted part of life.

Inevitably the conversation with Janet turned to father and brother Andrew who were living together in Edinburgh. Each would be grappling with the future direction of their lives, neither wanting to desert the other. Janet advised that Andrew did have a lady friend and father at age sixty six was still working but had handed most of the responsibility of the business to his partner. Although we were both concerned about the dilemma they would be facing we agreed that their future was their own decision. It was up to us to make it clear to them that they would both be welcome wherever we were living. We later spoke to Ann about this and she agreed with the sentiment.

All of this activity with family helped me to forget the marriage episode with Sarah. On my next visit to Melbourne Sarah and I spent some time together. There was no spark in the relationship and we both recognised this. Sarah had settled into a life fluctuating between her sister in Melbourne and her friends in Geelong. She spoke about her parents who had been in ill health and it was not a surprise when her sister Hannah told me later that she had gone home to look after her parents. I was able to bury my disappointment of a failed marriage in the sharply increased business activity at the Port. It was the arrival in Australia of my two sisters that reawakened my desire for a family life of my own.

It took father another nine years to book his passage on SS Great Britain to Australia. By this time, I was married to Agnes and our first child, Florence, had been born and died six weeks later of consumption. Our second child William Alexander was a baby and we had high hopes for him at that time. It was as well that we did not know what was ahead of us. Janet and Ann also had children during that nine-year period and I am sure that the desire to see his grandchildren was the incentive for him to make that physically difficult journey at the age of seventy three. In Gippsland, father lived alternately with Ann, Janet and me. He became an active member of the Presbyterian Church in Port Albert and was elected an elder within a year of his arrival. I am sure that the joy of living with his grandchildren for the last four years of life repaid him for the arduous journey to the antipodes. I am eternally grateful that his death preceded the tragic diphtheria epidemic of 1872.

After father came to Australia, Andrew married Margaret Liddle and eighteen months later he booked his passage on the "Southern Ocean", arriving in Australia in February 1865. The family were together in Sale when father died a year after Andrew arrived.

Andrew practiced as a solicitor and accountant in sale and we became close friends as well as being brothers. He had his share of sadness when his wife decided that life in Australia, far from her homeland of Scotland, was too difficult and she committed suicide. He later married Lucy Abbott and enjoyed eight years of married life before Lucy died six years before his own death in August 1894.

Is it natural for your first investment in property to have a special place in your heart? "Green Hills" was my first venture into property and it was one of the first freehold land purchases taken out of the Reeves survey in 1844. I did not finish payment for the property until six years later when I built a house on the hill. We all referred to "Green Hills" as the ridge of land near Tarraville, the highest area in what was otherwise a flat coastal plain. After I purchased the thirty two acres and built the first house my property became known as "Green Hills". I originally had only one house and my first tenant was Dr Hedley whose wife would prepare soup and make clothes that she would take down to the Tarraville bridge and give to the Aborigines.

It was not convenient for me to live at Green Hills while all of my business activity was down on the wharf area of Port Albert, but I subsequently built a second house on the rise to the north of the first house. This I lived in occasionally until it became a victim of a bush fire some thirty years later. Janet and her family lived in it for a short while and Anne and her family lived in it for a year while Spence decided on the best location to serve his large parish of the Free Church. During this period Anne and I nearly fell out when she wanted to send her daughter, Jessie, to Melbourne on a Cobb and Co Coach. I said "are you trying to kill the girl", a statement that Jessie remembered as she thanked me much later for winning the argument with her mother. She travelled more comfortably by ship to Melbourne.

My second tenant was John Pettit who was a surveyor and architect who designed the Christ Church and other Tarraville buildings. He showed me a letter that he had written to his family describing Green Hills and I asked him if I could use his description to advertise future rentals. I only had to show a copy of this letter to potential tenants and I had an immediate sale. This is what John Pettit wrote.

"This place Greenhills is by far the prettiest spot throughout the lower district of Gippsland. The house and garden are large and the verandah quite grown over with rose trees in full blossom – a wicked sentimental looking verandah – situated quite in the bush about two miles distant from Tarraville. I have several times been lost coming out at night from missing the track and on two occasions did not reach my destination until next day, spending the night amongst the scrub"

In addition to the two houses the property had outhouses, a stockyard, milking bails and a horse breaking pen and these additions made it easier to rent as a working farm. After a few short term tenants, I rented the property out to the Ray family who have continued to rent it until now. *(The property was sold to the Ray family in 1901 for 150 pounds and 4 shillings, to be paid off over a period. The title was finally passed over to James Ray on 11th June 1903)*

Ian C. Howden

Greenhills in 2012

On the Tigers Back

I was involved in the first steps of developing Gippsland through the gateway of port Albert. At first mine was a minor role but my first real step on the ladder to success was when Robert Turnbull put me in charge of the hotel that the Turnbull company had purchased at Port Albert. I am sure that the appointment was the result of the way that I had tackled the earlier responsibilities at Turnbull and Orr. My father had taught me that honesty and integrity are paramount in all of my endeavours and this has carried me through my life. I considered it of paramount importance to pass this recipe for success on to my children.

When given the responsibility of managing the hotel there were no licences until Commissioner Tyers came to the district three years later. In the intervening time I learnt how to brew beer and make soft drinks for sale through the hotel. These were profitable side lines of my own design and for my advantage. With the granting of the licences the brewing of beer became a legal activity and I held this licence for four years before relinquishing it. I maintaining a financial interest in the hotel with Robert Turnbull as the major shareholder.

When the Tara Vale Hotel was built I successfully applied for the licence so that for two years I held the licence for both hotels. The Tara Vale Hotel was opposite the Christ Church and close to the Tarraville bridge where during my tenure as licensee the Roads board set up a road toll. Unfortunately, the positioning of the toll gate beside the hotel gave the appearance of a conflict of interest and I relinquished the licence soon after being elected to the Roads Board. Until the formation of the board, the term "road" was a misnomer as the only well-formed roads were in the Port Albert vicinity. Once you proceeded more than half a mile out of town there were only tracks that soon petered out to ruts left by carts as they jolted to the residence of some remote settler. The first road the board completed was the water supply route from Tarra Vale to Port Albert commencing near the Tara Vale Hotel. Owning the hotel was another possible conflict of interest.

Most roads were formed by laying tea-tree longitudinally and transversely to the depth of about 18 inches. Large drains are excavated on each side and the soil thrown onto the layers of scrub. The roads formed in this way never bog but they require constant attention. The first major road was from Port Albert to Sale and was constructed with the help of convicts who were housed at Tarraville. Convicts crushed the rock from Wilson's Promontory for road building.

The composition of the board was an unwelcome thorn in the side of some of the outlying settlers because the board consisted entirely of publicans and shopkeepers who the settlers considered were favouring their own interests. The Roads board did a lot of good work building bridges and major roads but as well as the conflict with outside pressure groups there was conflict within the board. My first election to the board was soon after my marriage to Sarah and on reflection both were bad moves and both were not easy to shed. After seven years the roads board was replaced by the Alberton Shire council for which I successfully stood for election on three occasions.

The biggest single business in the district was carting and this had expanded rapidly with the discovery of gold. A number of enterprising men sorted out ways to enter the carting business. They needed help from the Turnbull and Howden company as we controlled the whole wharf area including the bond store and the warehouse. I was able to give them advice on conducting their enterprise and if the individual showed promise as a businessman I would help them financially. In this way I became a partner in some small carting enterprises. As new gold fields were developed pressure on the carting businesses increased and the horses were absorbing more work than was good for them.

Horses were a necessity for the future success of our trading businesses. The carters were not the only ones to need them, the settlers needed them to help clear the land, the roads board required sturdy horses, the drovers needed light horses and there was a demand from the goldfields for strong horses. I therefore took the initiative to import a Clydesdale stallion from Scotland. It was not a surprised when the response to my advertisement to mate my Clydesdale was rushed. My knowledge of breeding Clydesdales was limited to say the least, but help from my Scottish friends resulted in a fine Clydesdale stallion arriving at Tarraville. He was ready willing and able to satisfy the desires of mares owned by almost every draft horse owner in Gippsland. And he did not let me down.

GENERAL STORES.

PORT ALBERT.   3·03

IMPORTED CLYDESDALE HORSE.

THE undersigned expects the arrival, in a few weeks, of a first-class Clydesdale Entire, selected in Scotland by Mr. W. Pearson.

Parties wishing to improve the breed of draught stock in Gipps Land are requested to note the above.

The Horse will stand for the season in the neighbourhood of Tarraville, as soon as he is in condition after the arrival.

Further particulars in a future advertisement.

WILLIAM HOWDEN.

Tarraville, 2nd Oct., 1856.   9·0

YOUNG LINCOLN.

TO cover this season at the station of the undersigned the draught Stalion.

"Mother Buntine" became a partner in another small trading venture. She had lost her husband and was left to bring up three young boys. Her reputation was enhanced when, aided by her not inconsiderable frame, she flogged a drunken ruffian with her bullock whip for insulting a young girl. She was a hearty soul who was always good to talk to and was a great dance partner. At social events she would push you around the floor as if she was walking the baby in a pram. By the time the highland fling came plenty of liquor had been consumed and Mother Buntine would bounce her way through it with every part of her large body bouncing

The Old Store in 1860s and as it was in 2011

to the tune of the bagpipes. In the commercial world I was able to assist her by setting up a trading business with the outlying community. I am pleased to say she operated vigorously and with success. My simple trading business that started so slowly was diversifying beyond my wildest dreams. I was well and truly on the tigers back and there was more to come.

Shipping had been part of the Turnbull empire while I was still with them in Melbourne and I had learnt the import and export business while working for them there. Port Albert was acting as a free port that allowed imported goods to be stored in the bond store without paying duty until the goods were paid for and withdrawn. My Irish friend, John Mullaly, who was working in the customs house in Melbourne had now gone out on his own as a customs agent. I developed a tidy arrangement with him when taxable goods arrived at Port Albert via Melbourne. With control of the bond store and warehouse, Turnbull and Howden were by far the largest shipping agent at Port Albert, so why not venture into owning ships as Turnbull and Orr did in Melbourne. My first ship was a sailing ship, "The Twins" of which I was part owner. Most of "the Twins" trade was between Port Philip, Launceston and Port Albert. My next venture was to buy "The Ant", a small steam-ship trading mostly between Adelaide, Port Philip and Port Albert, and then another steamship "Despatch". Nothing like keeping up with modern technology.

Port Albert had the first bank in Gippsland and I invested heavily in it and lived to regret the trust that I placed in the banks never to lose money. The Bank of Victoria built its first bank in Victoria St, just a few houses from my home. At first it was a novelty to see the special gold coach arrive with a strong police escort. As time progressed it became a regular occurrence and the novelty of watching the gold unloaded into the bank vaults wore off. If we were waiting for a bank robbery it never occurred. The bank site was used for only six years before a more substantial building was constructed. It was just in time to receive the largest single delivery of gold weighing 2100 oz (62.5 Kg.)

First Bank of Victoria in Victoria St Port Albert where WB used to watch the unloading of gold. It is also the street in which he lived.

The Bank of Victoria built during the gold boom. It is the building that Agnes and the young children sheltered in during the major fires. The building is now used as a museum

The volume of trade grew astronomically, and the companies that I had interests in grew with it. Gold had to be shipped out in special containers under guard, the movement of sheep and cattle continued to grow, as did the agricultural products, tan bark, tallow and dried fish. Heavy machinery for the gold mines, household items for the growing population, wine, spirits, beer and food were imported in ever increasing quantities.

Probably the only business from which we were excluded completely was the Chinese fish curing enterprise. The Chinese bought their fish from the local fishermen at Long Point where they salted the fish before either sun drying or pickling in casks. The point was across the bay from Shipping Point and it became known as Chinaman's Point. There were 14 or more Chinese men, dressed in Chinese fashion, displaying shaved heads and pony tails. They never failed to turn heads when they came to town. Indeed I found great amusement watching our staff when they came to purchase supplies in our store. None of the Chinese spoke English fluently and there was much pointing and unintelligible noises as each tried to say some words in the others language. When the Chinese left there were always gales of laughter as we relived the experience. I can imagine what stories they told when they went back to their camp.

Every two weeks a ship would arrive from Melbourne and boats would set out from Chinaman's Point, rowed in the standing position and facing forward, a curiosity to the local fishermen. The bags of dried fish and casks of pickled fish would be loaded onto the ship and supplies for the Chinese community would be unloaded. The ship would immediately sail back to Melbourne and the rowboats depart back to the fish processing operation. We found out that the ship belonged to a Chinese Merchant in Melbourne who paid for the passage of the workers at Chinaman's Point and they worked for him until the value of the passage was paid off. Some of the produce was sold to the Chinese population in the Gippsland goldfields and the rest was sold to the Chinese in Melbourne, Ballarat and Bendigo.

It appeared that our trade-associated business was isolated from the disasters occasionally experienced by the settlers. Drought, floods and fire ruined many a farmer, even the celebrated Angus McMillan who lost his home and cattle in a bush fire. He had to sell off other runs in an attempt to regain his fortunes. I was shattered by his death which occurred when he fell while leading some prospectors into the alpine country. He never recovered and died two years later. He had been a regular customer at Turnbull and Howden's store and I was honoured to be his friend, the true discoverer of Gippsland. As a councillor I initiated a movement to have a memorial built in his honour. I thought this in some way compensated for the thoughtless action of Commissioner Tyers who, to make way for his house, cut down the she oak that Angus had inscribed "*ANGUS McMILLAN 14-2-1841*".

Model of the Chinese Fish Curing Enterprise
in the Port Albert Museum.

There was always a danger of bush fires in the summer but the greatest fire of all was in 1884. The day started with a hot wind from the north that brought the smell of burning timber. Smoke soon reached the town until it darkened the sky and it became obvious that a huge fire was raging and travelling in the direction of the Port. All of the men left town to see what could be done to hold it back. I took James and Robert with me and told Jessie to stay with her mother to look after the young children. We headed out towards Green Hills knowing that the fire was headed in that direction. We helped the Rays release the stock from the paddocks and drove the stock in the direction of the Tarraville beach. It became obvious that we did not have enough manpower to save both houses and our efforts were concentrated on saving the main house that the Ray family were living in. Everyone worked frantically throughout the day and into the evening extinguishing small fires started by sparks. Wet hessian bags and branches from trees were our only aids to extinguish flames and smoldering leaves driven by the fierce wind. Our shoulders ached and we were choked by the smoke as we battled to save the buildings. Later in the evening the wind changed from a hot north wind to a southerly breeze that turned the fire back on itself. It was too late to save our second house on the rise and it did not need the boy's inspection to realise that there was absolutely nothing to save when the fire had passed. We did rejoice with the Rays' that the house that they occupied was safe.

While the men were out fighting the fire the women took control of life at the Port. As the fire came closer they could see that Alberton was in the path of the fire and some houses were destined to go. Agnes realised that their best hope was to get everyone into a stone building. The bank manager took some ladies and children into the bank residence which was part of the bank building. Agnes and Jessie took our children to the warehouse on the wharf along with some of the other mothers and their children. Others were ushered into the court house while some of the brave ladies took the pews from the Anglican church and placed them on the road when it became obvious that the building could not be saved. Some were busy putting out some spot fires started by the smoldering leaves and black smut driven by the north wind. The church roof came crashing down sending sparks flying that endangered adjacent areas while a lady in the know gasped that the insurance had lapsed.

While some buildings were lost to the fire, and there were more than a few burn victims, there was no loss of life. This was the worst bush fire in my lifetime and I wish that I could say that there were no others, but there were, and one that upset me most was twenty years ago that caused the ruin and eventual death of Angus McMillan.

The downward passage of the balloon was heralded by debate on a variety of methods of transport to and from Gippsland. It was only a matter of time before Port Albert, once claiming the exalted title of "Capital of Gippsland" and "Gateway to Gippsland", would be overcome by one or more of the alternatives in the debate. The decline in gold discoveries and production would let more air out of the balloon.

The first competitive action came by opening the sand bar at Lakes Entrance so that small ships could enter the lakes system and service Gippsland from Lakes Entrance to Bairnsdale.

The strongest competition was the rail line debate. The debate centered around rail links to Port Albert from Dandenong, either over the hills to Welshpool, or an alternative line down the valley to Sale and on to Port Albert. The arguments on all alternatives were strongly debated and many heated exchanges were reported in the press. The rail line to Sale won the day and was completed in 1879. The population in Port Albert and surrounds had been dropping for the past few years and the opening of the rail line accelerated the decline. David and Robert Turnbull and I knew the effect that this would have on our many business ventures and we laid plans to consolidate some and sell off others.

Once the rail line from Melbourne to Sale was completed transport of goods through Port Albert dropped off dramatically. The main business was now in heavy equipment for the goldfields, because equipment was not easily carried by rail. Shipping was rapidly converting from sail to steam and we changed our vessels accordingly. But the trade was not there to justify expanding any transport venture that could not be linked to the rail.

There was a bright side in these declining years as commercial fishing increased, as did recreational fishermen. Sailing as a social pastime attracted gala events that brought business to the town but it would never again reach the golden years of the 1850's and 60's.

Although I had bought some properties previously, the people leaving were selling at bargain prices and I was able to increase the number of holdings at very reasonable prices. It was also time to ask leaseholders of our properties in and around Port Albert to convert to Certificates of Title. Some of the larger plots of land were subdivided and sold off in smaller lots.

The Duncan Family (written by Shirley Howden)

Will persuaded me that the story of his life was not complete without the Duncan story. I am not sure if reminiscing on one's life is a good or a bad thing to do after William's death. However whichever it is I have decided to do so and to insert this into the memoirs that he has written . I had travelled as a young woman and had a happy marriage which was the basis for the rest of my life, during which there were times of great happiness and others of deep sorrow.

I was born in Sydney, the second daughter of Alexander and Caroline Duncan. My mother had come to Australia at the age of 17 as a bounty immigrant on the "Leyton", a ship which caused much controversy on its arrival. However my mother obtained a position with Mrs Blaxland for 10 pounds a year. My father came in very different circumstances as a cabin passenger from Leith on the "Midlothian", arriving at Port Jackson in 1836. His trip went by a long route going first to Hobart and then to Sydney the journey taking 6 months. It was interesting to note that the ship was armed. Three months after his arrival my parents were married at St James church in Sydney, and before long my sister Caroline was born, followed by me. In 1840 my parents took us and a servant to England on the "Union". Looking back it is weird to realise that my future husband had arrived in Sydney in 1839 as we were preparing to leave.

While in England, we journeyed to Glasgow to visit my father's family. grandfather James Duncan had 8 sons and 3 daughters. His wife, Agnes Hood, had died some years ago, and of their children only my father, Alexander, and his brother David were married. My father and his brothers were very proud of their mother's brother, uncle James Hood, who was present at the battle of Waterloo, as a member of the Highland Regiment, and suffered the indignity of a leg wound.

Father's brother, David, was a travelling man, having been sent to Dutch Guyana in South America by the company he worked for. He unfortunately became very Ill, and when well enough returned to Scotland, so it was there that he, my father and grandfather would have discussed Australia. David decided to emigrate, and in 1842 on the "Widgeon" he met Anna Cade - a romance developed, but he disembarked at Hobart while she went on to Melbourne with her family. Very soon Anna returned to Tasmania, Married David and had several children before coming to Tarraville in 1848.

As my father had already been to Australia, he decided he would go to America. In 1841 on the "Westminster" we arrived in New York. We were now 3 children, aged 3 years, 18months and 4 months, and had with us aunt Jane, one of father's sisters. Mother certainly needed help with us 4 children. In the 1850 Pennsylvania Census, our family had increased again. Besides myself, Caroline and Elza we now had Grace, Franklin and

Kate - all American. Eliza had been born in England, Caroline and I in Australia - we were becoming a league of Nations!.

In 1851 father took the oath of allegiance in the Pennsylvania Supreme Court and was now an American citizen - this process had taken since 1848 to come into effect.

It took grandfather Duncan about 8 years after we had gone to America for he and his grown up family to come to Australia on the "Reaper" in 1849. What an upheaval for them at their stage in life - the eldest was 38 and the youngest 20, and their elderly father, 9 in all and no one really knowing what to expect. David and Anna were back from Tasmania when they arrived, but grandfather and his family did not stay long in Port Albert area before going to Wurruk (near Sale) . Here they lived out their lives in a genteel manner - none marrying.

Father's business kept us in a good lifestyle in Philadelphia and mother kept having babies - George, Margaret and Florence. When father died in 1856 she was with 8 young children and no relatives nearby. Her own parents who were Londoners had been dead for years and her in laws were now in Australia. She had already been there, so why not try it again - with 7 daughters to marry off. She no doubt would need some family support. My brother, Frank, left America before us, travelling with James Broad, whose brother later married my sister Margaret. Mother and us girls arrived in Melbourne in 1857, I was 17 and being one of the older ones had to help with the younger ones on the voyages, so I was glad to be at the end of the long journey - We went to Port Albert because David and Anna were there and our grandfather not far away at Warruk. Since we had enjoyed a good education in America, Caroline and I started a small school for a short time in Port Albert and before long I was being woo-ed by the colony's eligible man - William Howden - a widower. We were married in my family home on a very cold and windy day, but we had a lovely family day. Besides my immediate family, William's sisters, Ann and Janet and their husbands were there, along with grandfather Duncan, his family and uncle David and Anna. Before long I was pregnant much to Williams delight, but our joy was short-lived as baby Florence died several weeks after birth. The next year two of my sisters, Caroline and Eliza, were married. William was elated with the birth of our son William Alexander and the arrival of his father James on the "Great Britain" in1862. For some years afterwards there were the marriages of several of my sisters and William and I had 5 sons and our daughter Jessie.

The biggest shock for us all was the marriage of our mother to David Fermaner in 1864. he was listed on their marriage licence as a single man - he had been married in fact and grown up children - he was divorced about 1862/3 - he was well known in Port Albert being very involved in the shipping and became harbour master.

Shortly after more of William's relatives arrived, this time his brother Andrew and his wife, Margaret Bogue Liddle. Now all of Williams family was here. Sadly William's father died the next year in 1866 - We had enjoyed having him among us for 4 years and he loved being in Australia with his family. He was able to spend time in Sale with Anne and William Logan and their family. Andrew also was in Sale.

I was kept busy with my children and the family occasions which I loved and fortunately most were in port Albert. Little did we know the sorrow to befall us in 1872 - Our eldest son died on 14th January, followed 3 days later by Franklin. The another week and Percy our baby, and 2 weeks later, Walter Henry, all of diphtheria. I cannot believe that we lived through it - William and I began to wonder who would be next. The illness was dreadful, but I cannot describe burying 4 of my children and the emotions created. I took Jessie, James and Robert away while the house was fumigated - after so many years with weddings and babies. However I went on to have 4 more sons, Frederick, Henry, Reginald, and Arthur. We were not finished with diphtheria yet as my sister, Florence died at age 21of this dreadful disease at our sister Caroline's home in Emerald Hill in 1874.

Our home was always filled with friends and visitors, not to mention the numerous relations - We lived a comfortable life, William kept busy with his business affairs and vast local activities. When William went to Melbourne on business, occasionally I was able to go - enjoying the couple of days at sea - The "Keera", "Ant", and "Stormbird " some of the ships that we used. I was always amazed how Melbourne was growing between my visits. Both of us firmly believed in education and supported the local school with both its academic and sporting activities, in fact with all of our children, probably kept it going!. Our sons, as they grew older chose their future paths, two of them in Agricultural college, one studying medicine, several in business, all making their mark.

Our daughter Jessie was a great help to me with my family and charitable activities. Jessie was a gifted musician - her father's sisters Jane and Jessie were musical and some of their compositions were published. Maybe that is where my children's musical ability comes from. My Jessie loves her music and plays regularly at various functions. She played at a concert recently for families of the people lost on the "Alert" where everyone perished.

Since her marriage to David Fermaner, mother often moved between the married daughters for short stays, viewing grandchildren. She was in Sydney with Margaret and Andrew

Broad when she died, a coincidence that her life in Australia should end where it began so long ago.

News came to us of the death of William's brother Andrew in Sale on the 9th of August 1894 - William had not been well for some time and this was a blow for him. I could see his health failing, and our sons came to see him, but even with constant care and love he died on the 11th November.

Jessie and I were like lost souls, and two of the boys stayed with us for a few days after their father's death, and then we settled into a new routine.

I have decided now to give up the house in Port Albert and live nearer to Melbourne and the boys. I have been here for so long and seen so many changes. It will be hard to leave my beloved William and the children in the Alberton Cemetery, but my memories will always be with me.

Agnes Elizabeth Howden died on the 9th of August 1896 after a short illness, aged 55

Port Albert and My Own Family

In 1893 the Banking Crisis occurred in Australia when several of the commercial banks of the colonies within Australia collapsed. During the 1880's there was a speculative boom in the Australian property market. Australian banks were operating in a free banking system, there was no Central Bank and no Government provided deposit guarantees. The Federal Bank failed on January 30 1893 and by May 11 commercial banks had suspended trading. This had a huge impact on the fortunes of WB Howden.

South Australia was the first colony to give women equal franchise with men.

Robert Menzies and H.V. Evatt were born. Gold was discovered at Kalgoorlie by Paddy Hannon

It was 1857, I was a Councillor on the Alberton Shire Council, and I was confident that I would soon be elected as Shire President. The same year the Duncan family arrived in Port Albert.

Caroline Duncan, a young widow with 7 attractive daughters arrived in the male dominated town of Port Albert. What made them stand out among the Scottish and English community was their American Accent developed from 16 years of life in New York and Pennsylvania; If I said that I was not immediately attracted by the interesting Duncan family I would not be telling the truth.

It was 19 difficult years since I first set foot in Australia Felix and 10 years since the tumultuous marriage to Sarah. My sisters, Ann and Janet, and their families had joined me in Gippsland and Port Albert was the centre of growth. Could the rewards for those years of hardship be heading my way, or could there be further disappointments?

The Duncan family became very active in church life, they were a big attraction at Sunday school, and their home became the centre for lusty sing songs round the piano. It was no surprise that the sing song evenings were well attended by young men who suddenly developed a singing voice. Agnes and her sister, Caroline, approached me about establishing a school, and as Shire President this was an easy task to fulfil. I was able to find a suitable building for them to start this venture and I was very impressed in the way that they managed the school and the lovely approach to the children who were a variety of ages. They had obviously been well schooled themselves in America and they brought this knowledge to the little school they started in Port Albert.

Agnes exhibited a real get up and go attitude that impressed me and this became a dominant part of my casual conversation that did not go unnoticed by my sisters. At first there was no thought of developing a relationship with Agnes because of our age difference, but as our contacts became more frequent we became attracted to one another. It seemed that we were in a magnetic field when we were in a social group together, both finding interest in the other's past experiences. My sisters quickly noticed this and encouraged the relationship, helping me to overcome the doubts about the age difference.

Life at that time was very full, I finished my first term as Shire President in July and although that reduced some of the pressure on my time, the pace of business associated with gold and agriculture quickened. I have explained this in more detail in previous notes.

The relationship with Agnes also quickened so that I eventually decided that I must approach Agnes' s mother asking that I might court her with the intention of marriage. I had wrestled with the memory of the marriage to Sarah, but this was very different. Sarah had come to Australia with her sister without any family connections in Melbourne. She had very little education and I introduced her to what was a very unstable situation at Port Albert at the time. Ten years had made a huge difference to the Port and the future of Port Albert. Both Agnes and I had family living close by and I had a house in town with a lovely property and a house at Green Hills. A community of families had developed, and although the ratio of men to women was still high Port Albert was nothing like the rough pioneering town of the 1840's.

It was therefore with confidence that I approached Mrs Caroline Duncan. On reflection I guess that Mrs Duncan had considered how she could have her seven daughters married, and she must have thought it strange that I should ask the hand of her 18 year old daughter when Caroline and I had been born in the same year and we were both 43 years of age. She would have seen that Agnes and I were attracted to one another so that my confidence in a positive reply was well founded. We were married in 1859 on a very cold day in June. I do not know why the weather is the first thing that comes to mind. Maybe because my two sisters and the seven Duncan girls took over all of the arrangements. The church was decked out in Scottish, American and English decorations with greenery and any flowers that could be gathered in June. Agnes flowed down the aisle like an angel in her veil and dress made by the girls. We had booked out the hotel for visiting guests and the reception was held in the main dining room.

There was Scottish dancing to the bag pipes and ballroom dancing that filled the floor, with men in their dress suits or Sunday best, and the ladies in long graceful dresses. The celebration continued into the small hours of the next day, it was a wonderful time that lives in our memories.

The next step was to make our marriage work. Since I left Scotland 21 years ago I had only to think of myself, and to my shame I thought that I could continue in the same way. Agnes had stepped from a family reliant on one another for support and I had developed a strong sense of independence. I had accepted a second term as Shire President and a third term two years after that.

Agnes, photographed about the time of her marriage to William

At the same time, I became an equal partner in Turnbull Howden and Company, controlling all of the rapidly growing shipping trade through Port Albert, owning three ships as well as being involved with much of the community life of Port Albert. Agnes was often at home alone while I was attending meetings and business. On more than one occasion, between our marriage and the arrival of our first born, we did take the opportunity to visit Melbourne where I could mix business with pleasure

Agnes of course was no stranger to sea travel and a pleasant diversion to Hobart en-route to Melbourne gave us variety. I could not say that these were carefree trips but it was a new experience to have Agnes with me and we did enjoy further celebrations of our wedding with friends in Melbourne.

The "Twins", one of the three ships owned by WB used for trading between Port Albert, Launceston and Melbourne.

photograph in the Port Albert Museum of the Captain and Crew of the "Twins" one of the trading ships owned by WB.

At this time, we were living at Greenhills and I did enjoy the time away from the business world in town. Our first child Florence, arrived at the end of March 1860 when I was very involved in Shire council preparations for the elections in June and Just one year after our marriage. A few days after her birth, Florence developed a baby cough that turned the euphoria of having our first born into concern when the coughs produced phlegm. The doctors advised that there had been recent cases of consumption (more recently called Tuberculosis) in our district, and our concern turned to fear when after 2 or 3 weeks the phlegm was tinted with blood. She lost interest in suckling her mother's breast and was obviously in pain. To cry was her only way to convey to us the pain that she felt and we were helpless to do anything except comfort her in our arms until she went limp with exhaustion. For the next three weeks the wee babe struggled for breath to fill congested lungs, and cried with pain that spread throughout her tiny body. Agnes lived every minute of that time desperately trying to feed her, love her into living, but eventually, on May 7th Florence gave up the fight for life. Agnes had given everything in her efforts to save Florence and now she had to find a way to cope with the lost dreams of nurturing her own child.

As was the custom, the family members prepared the grave for burial. As I was rowed by friends up the Tarra River to the Alberton Cemetery, I wondered if there could have been anything that I should have done to save the beautiful daughter that we wanted so dearly to love. I certainly felt the loss but my heart was torn more by the obvious devastating sadness of Agnes. A man can bury himself in his work, which is exactly what I did, but Agnes had dreamt and planned about nurturing a baby through childhood for 9 months. Just like when a bubble that bursts, the dream left nothing for Agnes except the memory of a long pregnancy, a painful birth and shattered dreams.

There certainly were many hugs and questioning why, and how could it, and what if, but not until the diphtheria epidemic in 1872 and the loss of 4more of our children did I fully empathize with Agnes and her feelings at the loss of Florence. We were not coping alone, for family and friends were very supportive. As time would tell we had much greater losses to contend with.

When Agnes was expecting another baby the overwhelming sadness made way for expectation again and the expectation was realized with the arrival in January 1862 of William Alexander. Named of course after his father and grandfather. The fears of early infections passed and William grew into a lad for us to be proud of as our eldest son.

In June 1863 we were blessed with the birth of Jessie Balleny. Agnes really blossomed now with a son and heir and a lovely daughter to soften the memories of the loss of Florence. This was the first one of the grandchildren that my father was able to welcome to this world. He arrived in Australia soon after the birth of William, and with our two plus Anne and Janet's children about him he soaked up the joy of being a grandparent. Something he would not have been able to do if he remained in Scotland.

The arrival of William and Jessie and the excitement of father deciding to come out to Port Albert led me to reassess my priorities in life. I had been unhappy with the direction of the Alberton District Road Board. There was conflict between members of the Board and outlying farmers who complained that too much money was being spent on roads close to the towns to the detriment of the outlying areas; and they had a point. This was the main cause of conflict within the board and I made a conscious decision to absent myself from meetings which I knew would mean that my position on the Board would lapse. This was evidence to Agnes and the family that I was prepared to change my ways and would spend more time supporting their interests.

The front entrance at Greenhills.
Photographs taken by Trevor Howden in 1991.

At the time of Jessie's birth, we owned our house in Victoria St and the farm at "Greenhills" and a number of properties that returned good rents. The store at port Albert was a good source of income and I had good staff running it. The shipping business in partnership with Turnbull was operating profitably and was well managed. In short we were able to live comfortably now and I could look back with some pride at the results of the pioneering efforts since 1841. Some of the success was attributed to the changes in government during this period. Victoria was given separate colony status by the Parliament in England in 1851and graduated to self-government in 1856. These were important decisions for it shortened the lines of communication with government authority, and business progressed at a rapid rate. Port Albert competed with Melbourne as the busiest port in the new state of Victoria and the variety of Howden and Turnbull companies kept pace with the growth of the state.

After the arrival of William and Jessie Balleny, we were blessed with James in 1865, Franklyn in 1866, Robert in 1868 and Walter in 1870. Agnes was a great mother who organised the children and me with great affection and love. The church was the centre of much of the social activity where the town and the farming community mixed. The children all rode horses at a young age and were soon introduced to sailing and other sports including cricket for the boys. They spent a lot of time with their friends on our own farm and on friend's farms, and I often came home in the evening to find our six plus a variety of others under Agnes's management. Her time as a school teacher proved to be of great benefit.

Before the children attended school Agnes had taught them some early lessons so that they always got off to a good start when school days arrived. William was due to start his 6th year in 1872, Jessie was in year 5 and James in year 3. They were all bright children, always well up in their class and they all had an interest in sport and other outdoor activities. The three eldest owned a pony that they rode to school at Alberton and when Franklyn started in the early years of 1871 he rode behind Jessie or William on their ponies, their school bags over their shoulder, the three of them as one whether the pony was in a canter or at a trot. Franklyn had been promised a pony for his next birthday and I wish that I could have seen the four of them ride off together. Franklyn was so proud of his older siblings and at the age of 9 Jessie was so caring of her young brother. She would intervene when the boys engaged in some rough games at which Franklyn had not yet learned that he was not welcome yet. Jessie and Franklyn had developed a lovely relationship in spite of their age difference.

The arrival of Walter did mean a greater work load on Agnes but Jessie enjoyed looking after the babies and Franklyn was also a very responsible helper. Franklyn, Robert and Walter made a happy group at home with Agnes, and with three children at school it was a joyful phase in our lives to reflect upon.

Nothing could prepare us for what was soon to follow.

14

The Greatest Family Challenge

*In December 1872 the Victorian Parliament introduced the
first public central school system in the world based on the
principles of free, secular, and compulsory education.*

During the year I made a trip to Melbourne and devoted much
of my spare time there buying Christmas gifts for all of the
family. Agnes was pregnant again and we all looked forward to
have a brand new member of the family before Christmas. The
family were enjoying life at Green Hills and Agnes could not
have been a happier mother as she prepared for the birth. The
only concern was that a couple of the children had developed
a bad cold or 'flu, which was unusual for the summer months.

The school closed for the summer break with many of the
children sick with the "summer 'flu". William was the first of
our children to contract the sickness. It was not long before his
glands swelled and his breathing became laboured. When we
heard the doctor's chilling statement "I am afraid that he has
joined some of his school friends with diphtheria" it left us to
imagine what was ahead of us. The only treatment prescribed
was " To help the lad in his struggle to fill his lungs I recommend

that you fill a bowl with boiling water, add some eucalyptus oil and inhale the steam. Make sure that you cover his head and basin with a towel"; It was not pleasant. The odour of eucalyptus spread throughout the house as if to emphasise an atmosphere of sick children. The relief was only partial and did not last as the glands swelled and gradually blocked the air passages. The Christmas holiday period that had started with such promise had now converted our home in Victoria St into a hospital. By Christmas William's symptoms were well developed and Jessie and Franklyn were in the early stages, with eighteen-month-old Walter soon to follow. It was cruel to watch the heaving chest of such a strong young lad as William as he struggled for breath. The younger ones fixing their pain filled eyes on you, pleading for help. By new year the four of them were suffering the head under towel treatment for long periods, and baby Percy joined them. All five of them were striving to get air into an air starved and pain filled chest. But eucalyptus vapour was not the only thing fighting the life threatening disease. Agnes moved through the house with the vapour treatment, specially prepared liquid food and most of all encouraging words and cuddles.

It was only three weeks since the birth of Percy who was crying for attention and life, his mother not back to full strength after the birth. Agnes moved first to Walter not yet two, then to Franklyn five, Jessie nine and William ten, they all needed mother twenty-four hours a day. James aged seven and Robert, aged four were the last to join the children in their fight for life. It was a hospital home with mother and nurse Agnes fighting for the life of her seven children. At night we were on our own attending to the pleas and cries from the children who were not able to sleep. At daylight we both struggled to overcome our own lack of sleep to face a repeat of the same during the day. Florence, the youngest sister of Agnes was a great relief nurse and she was on hand most of the time to fulfil the necessary chores of cooking, cleaning and washing. Some of the members from our church also gave support in a number of ways.

January the 14ᵗʰ was the day that William gave up the struggle to fill his lungs. We found him in his bed with his face contorted in his final struggle for air. He was a brave lad to the end: he always wanted to live up to his position as the eldest son and heir. There was however little time for grieving as by now all of the children were in various stages of the dreaded disease.

As is the custom I went to the Alberton Cemetery with a couple of friends to dig the grave for the burial on January 16ᵗʰ. Even after preparing the grave my mind was still in an another world. The death of William had not been absorbed into my numb brain until I opened the door of the room in which he had slept. On the floor was the cricket bat and ball that he had received with such excitement at Christmas, and I remembered his words "We will have a game as soon as I am better". The bat and ball remained unused.

There was no time to absorb the fact that we had lost our eldest son who stood tall among his peers, and during his 10 years had made us so proud. Agnes was occupied with the baby Percy and dear Franklyn was gasping for breath and needed comfort. I did not know how to answer his question "will I go to live with Jesus like William?" I comforted him as well as I could, not knowing that the day after William's funeral his question would be answered.

On the road back to Port Albert from the Alberton cemetery where for the third time I had prepared a burial place for one of my children, my mind galloped between the children that we had buried and the five that we still had to save. Every one of the children were suffering and there was no way to control the inevitability of more deaths. In all of the difficulties I had encountered since I left Edinburgh 33 years ago I had never had one that was so hopelessly out of control. But it was far from over and I had to help Agnes to hold our family together. Baby Percy followed Franklyn the same way a week later and this effected Agnes more than any of the others. She had fought so hard to keep her 6 weeks old baby Percy alive.

The doctor was a friend of the family and we became aware of the unreasonable demands on his time. He was constantly in demand by distraught parents who had children fighting for breath and life throughout the Port Albert District. He had visited us the day before Percy died, and there was no medication that he could dispense for any of the children," just the same towel and eucalyptus vapour, as much as you can without distressing the baby" . This was his instruction as he rushed off to the next home.

As Agnes laid the lifeless Percy in his cot, she turned and said "Six weeks. The age of Florence, when she died". It was a comment of a mother shattered from the loss of 4 children and she had not forgotten the loss of her first child 12 years ago. A mother who came straight from the birth of Percy to nurse seven sick children. Her mind and body had withered under the pressure like a flower during a long hot day. I sat down and Agnes collapsed onto my lap and together we wept tears of despair. My tears as much for her as for the loss of the children.

When would we lose the next?

The answer came just 24 days later when Walter the 20-month old toddler with the big smile lost his battle for breath, and went with the others to Jesus.

Jessie and James recovered much faster than Robert who battled for some months before he fully recovered. he was now our youngest of the three surviving children and Jessie was now the eldest. The doctor recommended that the house be fumigated and while this was done we stayed a few days at a small inn called "Lily's Leaf". I thought that this was more appropriate than accepting the invitations from our friends. It also gave the 5 of us some space and time to grieve together.

Shortly after, my sister Anne invited us to stay with them in Sale for a week. This we accepted and it turned out to be a valuable healing time together with the Login family.

Agnes and 9-year-old Jessie had a very close mother daughter relationship and together they mothered Robert who was then 4 years old. The seven-year-old James and I had many opportunities to converse over the things in our heart. Although he was only 7 years old I started to introduce him to as much as I could of the business and the community activities in which I was involved. The disastrous start to 1872 for our family set a new direction for all of us. My life, until this disastrous month, had been building and accumulating assets. The immediate future required a healing period for all of us, and then plans for the next stage of our life.

Agnes was 32 and I was 51, we still had a lot of living to do.

*The family grave and headstone at the Alberton Cemetery.
In the background is the river which was used to
transport the coffins to the cemetery in a rowboat.*

Agnes was expecting again soon and Frederick was born in 1873, Henry two years later, Reginald after two more years and finally Arthur who was born in 1880.

As I write this more than 20 years later Agnes and I still find that something will trigger a heart wrenching memory of the children we laid to rest in the Alberton Cemetery. Our glances reveal that we immediately know the other's mind. The heart ache can only be relieved by the closest of embraces. We shed a tear and know that we can continue only by family unity and love. The ache from deep in the heart passes and life goes on.

The Children growing up

Although Jessie had been able to match it with the boys both intellectually and physically her reaction to the events of 1872 differed from James and Robert. She withdrew from the games of cricket and the horseback adventures in the district. After her schoolwork her personal interests became the piano and the violin. Agnes encouraged these interests that were the same as her own, and in the evenings they would play duets on the piano. Their musical talents were in demand at the church, for the church services, and whenever young friends gathered for fellowship in a friend's home.

The arrival of Frederick, Henry(Harry), Reginald and Arthur meant that there was a baby for Jessie to cuddle or console every day of her school years. Her pony was always the first out of the school yard, leaving the boys to follow their interests with their school mates. Jessie to mother her young brothers. Agnes cooked a slab of cake for the children every day and when Jessie arrived home the cake came out of the oven and was iced before the boys arrived. Soon she was loving a young one in her arms or playing with more than one on the floor. Jessie had finished her schooling at the age of 17, the year that Arthur was born. Reg was still not at school and very soon Agnes and Jessie became the centre of the social scene. The two boys always with them until it was their turn to go to school.

The family spent a lot of their early time together on weekends at the second house at Greenhills. but social activities in town became more attractive as the children went to school and made friends in town. Greenhills was leased to the Ray family in 1870 and they continued to farm the lease. In town there was a racing club, a rifle club, sailing club, church social activities, the skating rink and more to satisfy the children as they blossomed into adulthood. Race days were one of the opportunities for the ladies to dress up and relieve the dull colours of men's suit. The big events for the year were the sailing boat gala days. The hotel down on the water front became the centre of fashion and the starting and finishing of events could be viewed from the verandah. An imminent gala sailing season would be enough excuse for Jessie and Agnes to visit Melbourne where they explored the fashion houses. On their return they would show off their new dresses and hats to us before joining the crowd who came from near and far to add to the movement and laughter surrounding the waterfront.

Port Albert Hotel   Mrs Wendy Pope

Port Albert Hotel on a Gala Day

There were young men who showed interest in Jessie but she has never been attracted to any of them. I suspect that as she grew older the memories of her three brothers and sister losing their fearsome battle with tuberculosis has shaped her decisions about marriage. Jessie is a very empathetic soul who will come to the aid of anyone in trouble.

Jessie was a prominent member of the local orchestra and last month she organised a concert to raise funds for the families of the "Alert" that was sunk off the coast at Sorrento. There was only one survivor from the disaster. Jessie played solo items on violin and the piano and young Harry contributed with a fine rendition with his cornet.

While Agnes and Jessie strengthened the mother and daughter bond, I was enjoying many proud moments with the boys as they developed into manhood. I had been able to start a cricket club before I was married and all of the boys joined the junior ranks as soon as they were able. James became not only a proficient cricketer but was prominent in the social activities of the cricket club. Their fancy dress cricket matches drew crowds of spectators as the cricketers dressed in creative costume. James delighted in organising a match dressed in HMS Pinafore costume and the team took the field to the tune of the Gilbert and Sullivan comic opera. He was a member of a minstrel musical group.

All of the boys were members of the Regatta Club and sailed regularly. James called his yacht "Resolute" and with the others competed in the gala days. Most of the races went out up Old Man Creek, around Snake Island and return down Midge Channel to the cheers of the crowds gathered near the hotel.

I believed that all of the boys should learn to handle firearms safely and we formed a rifle club for this purpose. In spite of the fact that safe handling of a rifle was the first lesson, James was the victim of a shooting mishap that could have been fatal. In April 1881 James joined the Bank of Victoria and after initial training in Port Albert he was transferred to Melbourne. We were sad to see our eldest son leave but it was a proud evening for the family when most of the town turned up for his farewell. At the age of 26 he had made an impression particularly with his peers who made sure that he would not forget his farewell. James continued with his cricket in Melbourne and made his mark at the Melbourne Cricket Club as captain of one of the junior teams.

When James moved to Melbourne Bert (Robert Charles) took over as the leading light among his peers. Everything that James was involved with, Bert excelled in, and he took on further activities in Port Albert and Yarram. He is a splendid cricketer, has a fine singing voice and led the Minstrel and Dramatic Club. I remember his role as Whanotee, the Indian chief in the play Octoroon. He was the perfect comic relief in the melodrama about American slavery. It was his mother with her American background and flair that created such a loveable Whanotee in Bert. Everyone encouraged him to re-enact the part at a fancy dress cricket match followed by a fancy dress ball.

Although he was frequently to be found at the skating rink I was surprised to see him participating in skating carnivals. As if there was not enough opportunity for the young men to mix and meet with the young ladies in the district, Bert and his friends would organise dances at the Alberton hall. He and a friend used to sail in their yacht "Willing", and they entered in the regattas with enthusiasm. His greatest regatta triumph came when with wildly waving hat and in full sail he acknowledged the cheers of the crowd as he passed the winning post first in the main event of 1889. He took great pleasure in the win because it was in his own yacht "Sirocco". Later the same year he left Port Albert to Jackaroo at "Benerembah" sheep station. "Benerembah" is a large sheep station on the Murrumbidgee near Hay and is owned by Sir George Bailey.

It was very humbling for me, and I am sure it was for the 22-year-old Bert, when the whole district turned out for his farewell. Speeches from ministers of the churches and presidents of the numerous organisations that Bert attended were made in glowing terms. When all of the toasts for a successful future were made, the Alberton Shire President rose and with praise and fine oratory presented Bert with a set of gold studs.

When Bert moved interstate we still had four boys at school. Agnes was excellent at helping them with their school work and Frederick, Harry, Reg and Arthur were always on the prize list.

A Young Robert Charles Howden.
He died at the age of 43

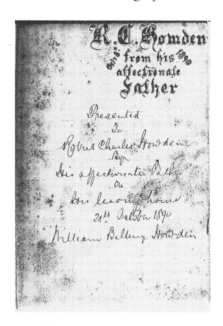

The opening page of the bible presented to Robert Charles when he
left Port Albert to Jackeroo at "Benerembah" sheep station near Hay.

Fred was dux of the Port Albert state school in 1886, Harry was dux in '89 and Reg was promoted up a class and was always the youngest in the class. This did not stop him from winning scholastic prizes.

Had the boys all stayed at Port Albert we could have entered a Howden cricket team in the competition. Fred displayed his talent very early and was chosen in the Port Albert men's team at the age of eleven. Music however was Fred's forte. Like his older brothers he was a member of the Minstrels and there was no concert without Fred playing the piano. The Presbyterian Church congregation sang lustily accompanied by Fred on the piano, and he was a member of the church choir. Even the Church of England called on his music ability to play the piano at a fund raising concert. The proceeds went to the installation of a shining new bell in the C of E grounds.

The ordered life of school came to an end in Fred's 18th year and he joined the Bank of Victoria as a ledger keeper. Promotion within the bank came after two years and he was transferred to the bank in the developing town of Bairnsdale in 1893.

Agnes and I were seeing the benefits of the change in direction since the 1872 devastating diphtheria period. The business activities had been well established by '72. The store, the hotels and the shipping business were all bedded down and they only had to be kept ticking along while I spent much more time supporting Agnes. For 2 years we restricted involvement outside our family and essential business activities, and we were supported by Agnes' sisters and the Trail and Login families. After that I became chairman of the Port Albert Regatta committee, a member of the Board of Advice for Schools in the District of Alberton, and on a number of committees in the Presbyterian Church. We bought a merry go round for the children and as they grew up we were able to loan it to charity functions in the district. Our concentration on developing our family with the Port Albert community was showing in the strength of character of our children.

Harry, Reg and Arthur still had to be nurtured into a life of their own. Harry probably had the best academic record at school and he would have followed his brother Bert into jackarooing if the new Agricultural College at Longerenong had not come to his notice. The college near Horsham in the Wimmera was established in 1889 by the Council of Agricultural Education. It did not require matriculation for entry and although Harry pleaded to go after second year secondary school we persuaded him to complete his matriculation which he did in 1893. I took Harry to Melbourne for discussions with the Council of Agricultural Education and enrolment at Longerenong Agricultural College.

The rail from Melbourne to Border Town had recently been completed with a station at Horsham. The original plan for us all to go to Longerenong with Harry to start the new year was changed when I fell ill. Agnes therefore took Harry with Arthur and Jessie and they boarded the train at Sale for the trip to Melbourne where they had an overnight stay. The 100 degree heat in late January made the Melbourne to Horsham trip very unpleasant. If they opened the windows to get some air they were covered with soot from the steam engine, and if they closed the windows the temperature became unbearable. It was a relief to be met at the Horsham station by members of the College and horses and buggy for the eight-mile journey to Longerenong.

For 14 year old Arthur the journey was not a problem at all, and on the return journey he was full of the potentially great life into which they had deposited his brother. For Agnes and Jessie the stopover day in Melbourne on the way out and back was the opportunity to indulge in the ladies sport of shopping.

While Reg and I were alone for a few days we talked about what he saw as his future. It is clear that he is academically capable of anything he chose, and his quiet nature is different from the other boys. A university degree looks like being the way that he will go and he has a year to work out what to study.

Following the journey with Harry to Longerenong, Arthur seems to have made up his mind to do the same as brother Harry. I would however like him to complete his matriculation first. He is an extrovert and very like Bert in many ways. He was chosen in the senior cricket team this year and he made some very good scores. Scholastically he won prizes in the primary school and is doing well in secondary school.

Our family at Port Albert had been reduced from nine to five and within two years it is likely to be down to three. Agnes is like any mother and as each of the boys left to make their life elsewhere she felt a part of herself had been transferred with them.

In the past we have discussed the possibility of moving, particularly when the rail to Sale was completed 17 years ago. This took most of the shipping business from us and made big changes to the business prospects in the district. But we had always come to the conclusion that Port Albert was a wonderful place to bring up the family.

Not long ago a visiting reporter from a Melbourne newspaper wrote about the youth in Port Albert "They are bringing up a fine race of people, in fact the fine physique of the young men and boys strikes the visitor. Several gentlemen told me that they thought a cavalry corps should be raised in the district about Port Albert for they were all excellent horsemen."

The decision that we made was justified by the strength of character of our children. I came to live in Port Albert fifty-two years ago and my sisters and my brother and my father all followed me out from Scotland. My sisters still live in the area and so do the sisters of Agnes. My father, and very recently my brother, Andrew, has been laid to rest in the district.

The decision to leave Scotland in 1839 has been justified and I give thanks to My God who has given me strength and guidance through my journey in life. I pay the greatest tribute to my wife Agnes who was able to rise above experiences that would have destroyed most women, yet she continued and passed on the fondest love to her children. They have responded in their own lives.

As my journey finishes I trust that they, their children and their children's children will continue the spirit that was carried from Edinburgh and nurtured in Port Albert.

Reg, Jim and Harry at the 80th birthday of Reg. On the tennis court of his house in Brighton

SOUTH GIPPSLAND CHRONICLE 13.11.1894

Mr. W.B.Howden who was a pioneer of half a century's experience in the South Gippsland district, and who was widely respected for his probity, geniality, and tact, both in business and in private life, passed through Death's portals last Sunday, at the honoured age of 79 years. The deceased, who was an uncle of Mr. A.W.Login of this town, and who leaves a wife and large family, most of whom are beyond the age of youth, was one of the early settlers of the Port Albert district, where he established as a general merchant and for many years carried on an extensive business throughout both South and North Gippsland. He continued in business till about 5 or 6 years ago, when old age began to assert its claims for consideration, and accordingly Mr. Howden ceased to take active part in conducting the trade of the firm, which has subsequently been managed by his son, Mr. J. Howden. The demise of this old resident removed one who made an extensive circle of acquaintances, and with few, if any exceptions, his straitforward dealings and kindly disposition in all matters of business, as well as in private concerns, was for him the greatest confidence, friendship and respect. At so ripe an age as 79, his death could not in some aspects be considered unexpected, but the departure from this life of one whose generous heart had levied a debt of gratitude on many who sought his assistance in troublous times will occasion warm feelings of regret amongst a large number of residents of this district and North Gippsland. Mr. Howden had for some time suffered from ill health and during the past three months had been confined to his bed, under the medical attendance of Dr. Birch, who, we are informed, certified that death was due senile decay. The remains of the deceased will be interred in the Alberton Cemetery this afternoon.

GIPPSLAND STANDARD 14.11.1894

IN MEMORIAN

The death of Mr. Wm. B. Howden which took place at his residence at Port Albert, on Sunday morning last, has removed yet another of the race of old pioneers, who have been privileged to see the land of their adoption rise into prominence in the early 50's and pass through various phases and stages — commercially and politically — during the three or four decades that followed. The subject of our present notice had the misfortune also to see Victoria thrust backwards for a time – Heaven knows for who long a period — through the collapse of many banking and other financial institutions as the result of the intensity of greed and gambling from which the land boom of 1888 was created. The late William Howden whose father was in a prosperous way of business as a jeweler in Edinburgh, was born on the 28th January, 1816. He consequently within three months of completing his 79th year, when called hence on Sunday last, after a rather protracted illness extending from the middle of September last. On the 15th September shortly after the death of his brother Andrew at Sale, Mr. Howden's absent sons were summoned by wire from Melbourne and Bairnsdale on account of the serious nature of his illness; for Dr. Birch held out no hope of his recovery. Dr Reid of Sale was then wired for, and in consultation with the local practitioner the decision was arrived at that the patient might pull through, although the age and the weakening condition were against him --- indigestion and its attendant troubles being the chief cause of his temporary prostration. But although the aged subject rallied considerably, and thereby inspired hope re his ultimate recovery, he did

The following Testimonials were printed in the South Gippsland Chronicle and the Gippsland Standard.

not regain sufficient strength to enable him to leave his room again. After 8 weeks illness, during which he was attended at short intervals by Dr. Birch, the final struggle came during Saturday night, and after a brief season of suffering early on Sunday morning the patient became calm and peaceful ere he sunk into sleep that knows no waking, and passed away quietly shortly before 10 oclock on the Sabbath morn. The deceased leaves a widow and seven in family to mourn the loss of a kind husband and fond parent, whose warm interest in the education and advancement of the young --- both socially and religiously---lead him to take an active part in connection with school prizes and childrens' sports until advancing age prevented further action, and increasing infirmity during the past 12 months of his life had the effect of confining his attention to the management of his business in the historical building which for over 40 years past has been known to the district residents as Turnbull & Howden's Store---although the other member of the firm died about 20 years ago. The subject of the present notice left Edinburgh and emigrated to Victoria in the year 1839, but did not take up his abode at Port Albert until 1842. Some years later on he entered into partnership with the late Robert Turnbull, who held a seat in the Legislative Council for the Gippsland Province for many years prior to his death. The firm of Turnbull & Howden at Port Albert was known and recognized by the settlers of Gippsland North & South in the early cattle shipping days as the most successful trading firm in the province; and after the death of Mr. Turnbull the business was continued under equally encouraging conditions until the opening of the railway from Port Albert to Melbourne in January 1892, when signs were not wanting that the oft-expressed opinion of Mr. Howden that the railway would "ruin the Port and District" was about to receive confirmation by the waning of business, thereby imposing a limit upon the hitherto satisfactory relations which had existed between the southern port and its several inland feeders. But no baneful or depressing influence worthy of the name presented itself in view until the bank crashed in 1893, when the estate of the now deceased merchant was affected to such an extent as to imply a reduction in his income of four or five hundred per annum. But time, and recovery of lost ground by the reconstructed banks---notably the Bank of Victoria in this instance ---may restore somewhat of the wealth that had been thus locked up, and thereby increase the value of the estate for the benefit of the widow and family. In addition to bank shares and hard cash the deceased gentleman held many valuable properties, in North and South Gippsland, including the Exchange Hotel at Sale and landed estates at Green Hills, Tarraville, Alberton East, Woodside and Port Albert, any or all of which may rise in value as a result of improved conditions of Colony and people towards the close of the nineteenth century. The deceased had relatives in the Colony and district outside his own family circle, his sister being the wife of the Rev. Mr. Login Presbyterian Minister of Sale; he was also related by marriage to Mr. David Duncan of Woodlands near Tarraville, who is also an old identity in the South and still in the land of the living. Although the amassing of wealth was undoubtedly one of the ruling maxims of his life, the name of William Howden to any document or business transaction was sufficient guarantee that there would be no default or breach of trust in connection herewith; whilst there was always a soft side or vulnerable spot to be touched in the cause of religion, charity and legitimate recreation by those who knew how to approach him in regard to such matters. He was a warm supporter of agricultural pursuits and was one of the foremost and most enthusiastic promoters of the South Gippsland Pastoral and Agricultural Association about thirteen years back. In fact he was one of the seven fathers of the Society—in association with Captain Slade, and Messrs. A. Bland, P. Brennan, D. Fraser, J. Rossiter and the late John Gellion. But a few years later on they left a real live institution to those younger and more active residents of the South who have taken up the running in the interests of this flourishing society on the more extended area at Yarram. Take him for all in all, the deceased was a genuine representative of the old time son of Scotia; for although he had a keen eye to the acquisition of wealth, he could be genial and hospitable to friends and visitors, and took pleasure in seeing other folks enjoy themselves---as witness his expenditure of time and money on certain occasions when school sports or other seasonable rejoicings were to the fore, and called for a little friendly assistance. At all events we can speak favorably of him as an old friend and fellow worker for district institutions in the seventies and eighties, a staunch upholder of the religion of his forefathers, and an all round honorable man. And when the numerous following of district residents committed his remains to the tomb where five of his children were laid twenty years ago, the feeling of esteem and respect for the memory of the deceased would be general and genuine. For it is not given to many men in this life to spend half a century in one place, and go down to the grave with a record for having withstood the enticing allurements which promised wealth untold, but left his widow and family in a position of ease and affluence notwithstanding the heavy drain upon his well husbanded resources through partial collapse of the banks. Having thus briefly and truthfully sketched somewhat of the life and history of the deceased, it only remains for us to add that the closing scene at the grave in the Alberton General Cemetery yesterday afternoon was witnessed by a very large number of district residents. The service at the grave was read in an impressive manner by the Rev. D. Telfer, Presbyterian minister of Tarraville, the conduct of the funeral being entrusted to Mr. M. Pearson, of Port Albert.

94 Descendants of WB Howden gathered in Melbourne in 2011

Printed in the United States
By Bookmasters